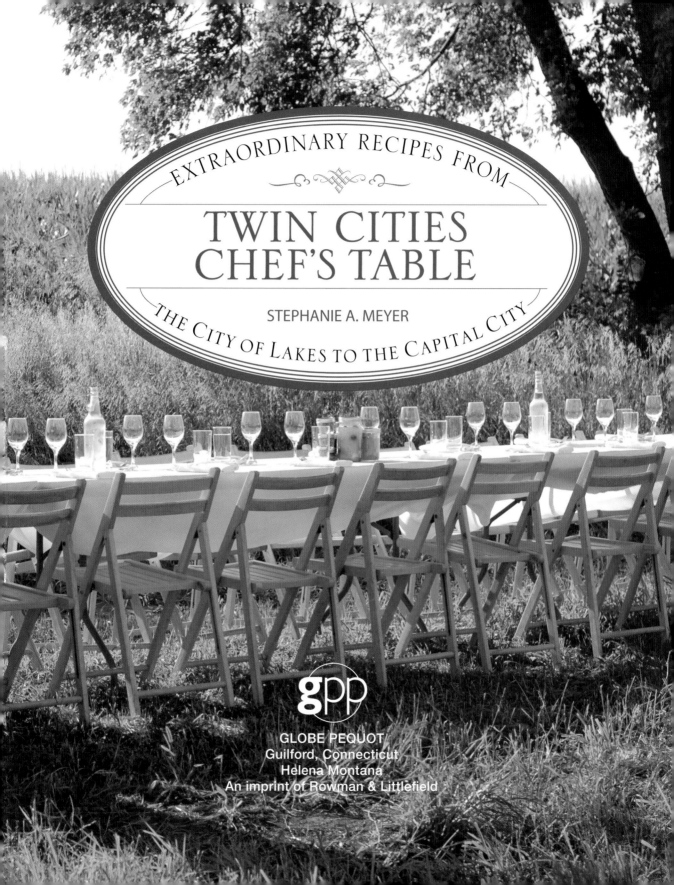

EXTRAORDINARY RECIPES FROM

TWIN CITIES CHEF'S TABLE

STEPHANIE A. MEYER

THE CITY OF LAKES TO THE CAPITAL CITY

gpp

GLOBE PEQUOT
Guilford, Connecticut
Helena Montana
An imprint of Rowman & Littlefield

Globe Pequot is an imprint of Rowman & Littlefield

Distributed by NATIONAL BOOK NETWORK

Copyright © 2014 by Rowman & Littlefield

All photography by Stephanie A. Meyer

British Library Cataloguing-in-Publication Information available

Library of Congress Cataloging-in-Publication Data available

ISBN 978-0-7627-9219-1 (hardcover)

∞™ The paper used in this publication meets the minimum requirements of American National Standard for Information Sciences—Permanence of Paper for Printed Library Materials, ANSI/NISO Z39.48-1992.

Restaurants and chefs often come and go, and menus are ever changing. We recommend you call ahead to obtain current information before visiting any of the establishments in this book.

For Nathan, off on new adventures.
Come home any time you like, and I'll cook for you.

CONTENTS

Recipes by Course

SOUPS & SALADS

Appetizers & Drinks

Sandwiches, Sides & Sauces

Main Dishes

Breakfast & Desserts

Acknowledgments

It's been quite a year. After committing last summer to working full-time on my food blog and business, *Fresh Tart*, I was contacted by Tracee Williams, acquisitions editor at Globe Pequot, about writing a Twin Cities edition for the Chef's Table series. After much discussion with my dear friend Zoe Francois, coauthor of the wildly popular *Artisan Bread in Five Minutes a Day* series of books, I decided to set my *Fresh Tart* plan aside and embark on the adventure of writing a cookbook.

At the same time, I started writing a monthly chef's recipe column for *Minnesota Monthly* magazine, called Cook Like, and all of a sudden my whole world was restaurants and chefs and their recipes. It's been a transformative experience of making new friends and connecting with old ones, learning more about my own cooking, and pushing my writing and photography in new directions. What a gift and opportunity to connect even more deeply with the Twin Cities food community.

And so, I must heartily thank Tracee, who has been a much kinder and more supportive editor than I deserve. It has been my sincere pleasure to work with her. I'm so grateful to Zoe for her advice, depth of knowledge, and generosity in sharing it, and for introducing me to Jane Dystel at Dystel & Goderich Literary Management, who has kindly instructed me in the ways of the publishing world as well as offering support throughout the project. I also want to thank Patrick O'Brien for his wise counsel and guidance all the way along.

When I took this book on, I knew I needed help—big time—and Angie Zirngible answered the call. Her project management experience was invaluable in gathering recipes, fact-checking restaurant names, and getting the ball rolling. I wish we'd been able to work side by side more often, because she is a lovely person.

To select the eateries included in the book—not an easy task—I made a list off the top of my head and then leaned heavily on my food-industry friends, the ladies of #L2, to help me narrow the field. But that's not all they did. I also thank them for recipe testing, gathering releases, sharing recipes, and scooping me from The Treehouse for sustenance, with a special thank-you to Joy Summers for her occasional photography assistance, but mostly for her creative genius and many hours of work on the project.

They were not the only recipe testers. Thank you also to recipe developers Emily Anderson, Laurie Jesch-Kulseth (thanks also to Laurie for her beer expertise), and Kate Selner for their cooking knowledge and excellent taste. I'm grateful to my friend and collaborator Chef Scott Pampuch for fielding many culinary and recipe-related questions, and to Andrew Zimmern, Daniel Klein, and Stephanie March for their insight into the Twin Cities food community.

I am lucky to be part of a collaborative and supportive food-blogging group known as Fortify: A Food Community. I thank them heartily for cheering me on, checking in on my progress, sending notes of encouragement, and offering assistance with recipe testing and editing. They are big fans of Twin Cities restaurants and chefs, and they are so excited to see this book. How cool is that?

The members of my family have been saints waiting for me to finish. I missed vacations, dinners, and holidays while I worked, and they supported me completely. Thanks in particular to my mom, who is always my number-one fan.

And, of course, I am so grateful to all of the chefs, restaurant owners, farmers, co-ops, and other purveyors who donated their talent, time, and recipes to *Twin Cities Chef's Table*, the way they donate their talent, time, and food to countless causes, events, and charities throughout the year. It has been an honor to photograph and write about you. Thank you.

Introduction

What is Midwest cuisine? It's a pretty hot topic these days, and not just in the Midwest. With pickling, preserving, pork, and pie earning the spotlight on New York and Los Angeles menus, and local chef-hero Amy Thielen's hit series *Heartland Table* winning fans on the Food Network, we're feeling a little bit famous right now.

But only a little. Humble is the Minnesota way, ya know.

Of course it's not just recently that Midwest ingredients have been appreciated on a national level. We're called America's Heartland for a reason—the Midwest in general and Minnesota in particular send best-quality meat, fresh dairy, artisanal cheeses, and heirloom grains all over the United States and the world. When I was teased as a child for living in the flat, cold Red River Valley, I would retort, "Yeah, well it's the breadbasket of the world!" I didn't know exactly what I was saying, but now I know that I was right.

I grew up in Minnesota, North Dakota, and Wisconsin, scarfing down signature Midwest foods: roasts, butter, freshwater fish, garden vegetables, cured meats, wild game, fruit pies, hotdish, and bar cookies. If you'd asked six-year-old me to name my favorite meal, I would have answered Green Lake walleye fried in butter. I still fry a batch several times a year because I believe with all my heart that fresh, seasonal food prepared simply with good butter is some of the best food in the world.

When I was approached about writing *Twin Cities Chef's Table*, the mission was to define Twin Cities cuisine as farm to table, with a vibrant ethnic food scene, highlighting chefs who are achieving national recognition. I checked that mission widely with local food industry professionals, media, and chef friends, and everyone agreed—it fits! To fill out the rest of the story, I included features about local farms, the co-op movement, public and farmers' markets, food trucks, and craft-beer breweries. Together they paint a picture of Minneapolis and St. Paul that is so much more colorful and spicy than our reputation for cold winters and comfort food.

When I arrived in Minneapolis in the early 1990s, large-scale fine dining was the name of the good-food game. Just a decade later, the scene had completely shifted. By the mid-2000s, white tablecloths had all but disappeared, replaced by smaller chef-owned eateries developing signature styles and applying big flavors to classic Midwest ingredients.

What fueled the transition? First were restaurateur brothers Larry and Richard D'Amico, who in the 1980s shook up the Minneapolis–St. Paul dining scene status quo with their focus on excellence. Executive Chef Jay Sparks joined their team in 1989, and many of the top local chefs trained in his kitchens and credit him for their success and for elevating the local dining scene.

And then there was the economy. The Travel Channel's *Bizarre Foods* host, Chef Andrew Zimmern—who has cooked and made his home in the Twin Cities for more than twenty years—notes that the economic downturn in the early 1990s hit the Twin Cities dining scene hard . . . in a good way. "People stopped trying to open 250-seat restaurants in downtown Minneapolis, and the fifty-seat, neighborhood restaurant was born." Smaller restaurants offered this new cadre of ambitious, well-trained young chefs the opportunity to flex their culinary muscles and to really know and build trust with their customers. Add to the mix an infusion of Latin American, Southeast Asian, African, and Middle Eastern immigrants and their delectable cuisines, the recent explosion of street cuisine via food trucks, and a rediscovering of the farm-to-table movement, and the new name of the good-food game is innovation.

And collaboration, according to Stephanie March, food editor of *Mpls.St. Paul Magazine*. "There's a sense of camaraderie among most of the chefs in town who have 'grown up' together that is really knitting an interesting landscape. The cooks who have been mentored by the top tier of restaurateurs are supported by the kitchens they leave. This creates a connective tissue among restaurants that helps make them stronger. If they know they can ask for advice or support from their ranks, it makes them a better independent force, and more likely to be able to survive the up-and-down cycles of the crazy world that is the biz."

You'll see all of these influences as you page through this book. It's an exciting time to be eating in the Twin Cities. No matter the cuisine, the combination of a strong Midwest agricultural tradition combined with our short growing season has meant a particular focus on seasonally driven menus. As Daniel Klein, cohost/coproducer of the documentary series *The Perennial Plate*, puts it, "The Midwest is a place where so many of the foods that we love shine for a brief but wonderful window. And while the bounty of our best vegetables and dairy and meat yields delicious eating in the season, these moments need to be preserved for the rest of the year, and that preservation yields equally delicious pickles, cheese, and bacon." It also yields fantastic beer, spirits, ice creams, and baked goods, so it isn't surprising that Minnesotans are falling in love with these artisan-made goods as well.

A hot food scene attracts talented media to spread the word, and the Twin Cities boast some of the best in the country. In addition to Thielen, Zimmern, and Klein, *The Splendid Table*'s Lynne Rosetto Kasper and *Mpls.St. Paul Magazine*'s Dara Moskowitz Grumdahl are all James Beard Foundation Award winners for their work. Stephanie March, Rick Nelson of the *StarTribune*, James Norton of *The Heavy Table*, Rachel Hutton and Joy Summers of *Minnesota Monthly* magazine, Jason DeRusha of WCCO-TV, and a passionate group of independent food bloggers are just a few of the fantastic storytellers shining a light on the people who grow and make what we eat and drink.

Where's it all headed? According to Zimmern, "Our chefs are achieving national attention, and national-caliber chefs are starting to open restaurants in the Twin Cities. This is not a blip on the radar." He sees continued opportunity for growth in the defining of a new Midwest cuisine. "When you say 'New Orleans,' you can taste it. That's not true for the Twin Cities, not yet. It will be interesting to see what the flavor turns out to be." *Stay tuned* . . .

The Bachelor Farmer

50 N. 2nd Avenue
Minneapolis, MN 55401
(612) 206-3920
THEBACHELORFARMER.COM
Owners: Eric Dayton and Andrew Dayton
Executive Chef: Paul Berglund

In Minnesota, we're fine with knowing we aren't exactly the hippest spot in the country. Trends tend to arrive a few years tardy, and despite being a hotbed for Coen brothers' movie plots, not many aspire to be us. That is, until they get a taste of what Eric and Andrew Dayton have created at The Bachelor Farmer and Marvel Bar. The restaurant space is quintessential Midwest, right down to the barn-wood floors, crocheted blankets, and country-blue be-hearted wallpaper, yet it somehow all feels modern, trendsetting, and decidedly hip. The Nordic-inspired food—both aesthetically clean and cozy comforting—matches the old-meets-new vibe in stunning form (just ask President Obama, who dined there in 2012).

Chef Paul Berglund is drawing national attention—including a 2014 James Beard Foundation nomination for Best Chef Midwest—with dishes almost too pretty to eat. Almost. The menu changes daily, but with dishes like duck (breast and confit) with black

lentils, roasted rutabaga, celery root, and pickled beets, or toasts topped with beef tartare, fermented sunchokes, cashew milk, capers, and horseradish, you get a sense of the depth of flavor and technique at play in Berglund's kitchen and of what motivates his menu and commitment to hospitality. "Family meals at the dinner table meant more to me than I could have imagined as a child. The food itself was simple and honest. It was the experience of eating as a family, however, that solidified my understanding of the relevance of food to the connection between people."

The fast-growing North Loop neighborhood of Minneapolis is keeping The Bachelor Farmer's beloved weekend brunch packed with late-rising young professionals who probably sipped a few cocktails the night before at Marvel Bar. Bar manager Pip Hanson is at the crest of the Twin Cities' craft cocktail revival, drawing attention from around the world for his marvelously—pun intended—sophisticated drink program. While most mixologists are rediscovering the classics, Hanson is busy inventing new ones. Rather than simply serving scotch straight up or neat, he infuses it with kombu, enhancing the peaty beauty of the spirit.

When the Dayton brothers—sons of Minnesota governor Mark Dayton—first announced their intentions to open a restaurant and speakeasy-style bar, a few skeptics wondered what they knew about running a restaurant. The result speaks for itself. In addition to the smash-hit restaurant, the restored, historic warehouse now houses one of the most in-demand event spaces in town, a chic clothing store, a rooftop garden that supplies the restaurant, and more Minnesota glamour than you can shake a stick at.

Duck Fat–Roasted Beet Salad

(SERVES 4)

Chef Berglund's note: Beets are so frequently cooked in the same manner (either simply boiled or roasted), that it's fun sometimes to do things differently and learn about another side of beets. Duck fat adds a richness to the beets that gives them a unique flavor; however, I don't see anything wrong with using a good olive oil as a substitute. The first five steps can be done up to two hours before serving the salad.

¼ cup rendered duck fat (ask your butcher or specialty food store, or order online)

4 medium-sized beets, different colors if possible, peeled and sliced ⅛-inch thick with a mandoline or sharp knife

1 tablespoon kosher salt, divided

¼ cup raw almonds

1 teaspoon plus 1 tablespoon grapeseed oil

1 medium shallot, finely diced

1½ teaspoons apple cider vinegar

Pinch of sugar

½ cup (½-inch cubes) pain de mie bread

1 tablespoon unsalted butter, melted

4 sprigs fresh parsley, finely chopped

Parmesan cheese, for shaving

Freshly ground black pepper (optional)

Preheat oven to 350°F. In a bowl in the microwave, or in a small saucepan over low heat, melt the duck fat.

Line a baking sheet with parchment or waxed paper, and lay the beets out evenly on the sheet. Brush beets lightly with duck fat, just enough to coat them, and sprinkle with 1 teaspoon kosher salt or to taste. Flip the beets over, brush the other side with the duck fat, and sprinkle with another 1 teaspoon salt. Place the beets in the oven and roast for approximately 10–15 minutes, turning them halfway through. Taste a beet for doneness: When done, it will still have a bit of a bite (not totally soft), a lightly roasted taste, and a few of the beets will have slightly crispy edges.

Remove the beets from the oven (leave oven on) and cool. (Sometimes white, gold, or Chioggia beets will have brown or black flecks in them after roasting. This is perfectly normal and adds to the color palate of the plate, in my opinion.)

While the beets cool, place the almonds on a baking sheet and roast 10 minutes or until lightly browned in spots (leave oven on). Transfer almonds to a small bowl, toss with 1 teaspoon grapeseed oil and ½ teaspoon salt. Transfer almonds back to the baking sheet and allow to cool. Roughly chop them and set aside.

Place the shallot in a small bowl and add the remaining 1 tablespoon grapeseed oil, vinegar, ½ teaspoon salt, and sugar. Let mixture rest for 15 minutes to mellow the raw heat of the shallot.

Toss the pain de mie bread cubes with the butter, spread on a baking sheet, and toast in oven until they turn a deep golden, stirring once, about 7–10 minutes (watch them carefully).

To assemble the salad, divide the roasted beets among four plates, making a mosaic of beautifully colored beets. Drain the shallots a bit, then sprinkle them over the beets. Scatter the almonds, pain de mie croutons, and parsley on top of the beets and almonds. Lastly, using a wide cheese shaver (or vegetable peeler), shave shards of Parmesan cheese over the plate to your liking. Freshly cracked black pepper would be wonderful, if you're in the mood. Enjoy.

BE'WICHED DELI

800 WASHINGTON AVENUE NORTH
MINNEAPOLIS, MN 55401
(612) 767-4330
BEWICHEDDELI.COM
EXECUTIVE CHEFS/CO-OWNERS: MATTHEW BICKFORD AND MIKE RYAN
SOUS CHEF: STEVE TENTIS

Be'Wiched Deli is part meat-and-sandwich shop, part magic. Owned by two fine-dining-trained chefs, every item of food they serve has been labored over. "We've spent our culinary careers in the kitchens of fine dining restaurants. Our polished technique and passion for quality ingredients inspired us to open a gourmet sandwich shop serving artisanal sandwiches, salads, and soups." No bite is more delicious proof than their signature pastrami: Tender meat perfumed with a heady mix of pepper and sultry spices melts the moment it meets your tongue. In the morning, they'll slap an egg on top, and there is no better place for your mouth to be.

The small shop in the now-bustling North Loop neighborhood was one of several restaurants that jump-started the revival of this warehouse-turned-condominium slice of town. When explaining how they settled on channeling their combined culinary talents into a deli, Chef Ryan says, "We all have to eat! Some people eat just for sustenance, others for the pleasures of that often-elusive balanced bite, plate, or meal. The pleasures that food can bring can be like a time machine. I remember eating a perfectly ripe strawberry out of my great-grandmother's garden (I was supposed to be picking them for jam!), still warm from the sun, the sandy soil under my toes, juice rolling down my chin. So simply delicious, so memorable. I take inspiration from times like my 'strawberry moment' and attempt to bring similar pleasures to others with good food. Whether it's some fat cat in a $1,000 suit, or a city maintenance worker, everyone loves a good sandwich!"

Be'Wiched serves scratch-cooked food memories to hungry diners at all hours of the day. You won't soon be forgetting that good sandwich delivered to your desk (by bike!), the sweet-and-smoky weekend brunch, or the hot bowl of soup washed down with a cold, local brew that restored you at the end of a long week.

WILD MUSHROOM SOUP

(SERVES 6)

½ ounce dried shiitake mushrooms

1 cup hot water

2 tablespoons olive oil

1 pound hen of the woods (maitake) mushrooms, wiped clean, broken into 1-inch pieces

8 ounces assorted fresh mushrooms

2 large shallots, minced, 1 tablespoon reserved for garnish

1 small leek, diced

1 small sweet onion, peeled and diced

1 stalk celery, diced

1 carrot, peeled and diced

1 medium potato, peeled and diced

8 cloves garlic, minced

2 bay leaves

2½ teaspoons minced fresh thyme, half reserved for garnish

1 teaspoon minced fresh sage

1 cup white table wine

2 tablespoons cognac or sherry

1 cup heavy cream

6 cups chicken broth

Juice of 1 lemon

Salt and freshly ground pepper

2 tablespoons unsalted butter

Sour cream, for serving

In a small bowl, soak dried shiitake mushrooms in hot water for 30 minutes. Drain mushrooms, discarding liquid. Chop shiitakes.

Set a dutch oven or other large, heavy-bottomed soup pot over medium-high heat. Add olive oil and, when oil is hot, add hen of the woods mushrooms and sauté for 5–6 minutes or until just beginning to soften. Remove and reserve 1 cup of the par-cooked mushrooms.

Add shiitakes, fresh mushrooms, and remaining vegetables and herbs. Sauté until vegetables are tender, about 15 minutes. Remove and reserve 2 cups of the cooked vegetables. Deglaze the pan and remaining vegetables with wine and cognac. When wine is reduced by half, stir in heavy cream and chicken stock. When soup boils, turn heat to low and simmer, uncovered, for 30 minutes.

Carefully puree hot soup in a blender, working in batches. Be aware that blending hot liquids requires extra care, so never overfill the container. Stir reserved vegetables into pureed soup and season with lemon juice, salt, and pepper. Keep soup hot.

In an 8-inch skillet over medium heat, add butter. When butter is melted, stir in par-cooked hen of the woods mushrooms, reserved shallot, and reserved thyme. Sauté mushroom-shallot mixture until mushrooms are tender, about 10 minutes.

Serve soup in warm soup bowls, topped with mushroom-shallot mixture. Finish with a dollop of sour cream.

Birchwood Cafe

3311 E. 25th Street
Minneapolis MN 55406
(612) 722-4474
birchwoodcafe.com
Owner: Tracy Singleton
Executive Chef: Marshall Paulsen

Birchwood Cafe's motto is Good Real Food, painted in cheerful letters right onto the windows of this welcoming neighborhood gem. Proprietor Tracy Singleton has worked for more than seventeen years to source top-notch, locally and sustainably sourced organic ingredients for the Birchwood. Whether you walk down the block for a tender, crispy savory waffle topped with a sunny egg and lardons, or ride your bike over for tofu hash loaded with fresh-from-the-farm vegetables, Birchwood Cafe's loyal customers count on eating ethically and deliciously.

Executive Chef Marshall Paulsen joined the Birchwood in 2007 and hasn't looked back. He's made a name for himself by cleverly balancing a sophisticated, seasonally changing menu with well-loved, comfy Birchwood classics. The formula is a winner in every way—for the more than forty farms whose bounty he works with and for the happy, healthy diners who keep the place hopping morning, noon, and night. For Paulsen, "There is no all-encompassing formula, road map, instruction, or text book that defines a good chef—creativity, passion, personal style, and relationships with farmers, coworkers, and guests contribute more to my ability to succeed and be successful as a chef than just technique alone."

However, Birchwood Cafe is more than Good Real Food. It's a neighborhood gathering spot, a place for parents to sip wine at a sunny sidewalk table while their children play hopscotch with Singleton's daughter, Lily. Paulsen and wife Amanda Layer's toddler daughter, Liesl, is at home at the Birchwood as well, as are the Birchwood Cafe bike team, the former mayor of Minneapolis and his family, first dates, book groups, and visiting real-food luminaries like Michael Pollan and Will Allen. The first time I stopped by the Birchwood was to pick up a dozen duck eggs a stranger offered over Twitter; we hit it off immediately and became fast friends.

In case you're tempted to roll your eyes at the oft-overused terms *local* and *sustainable*, know that Birchwood Cafe walks their talk, big time. Singleton, Paulsen, the staff, and friends are dedicated volunteers and activists for and on behalf of local growers and producers. Testifying at the capitol, organizing "crop mobs" to help with harvesting, and collaborating with Minneapolis public schools to improve school lunches are just a few of the ways that Team Birchwood works on behalf of the Twin Cities food community. And

the community approves: Birchwood Cafe recently wrapped a successful Kickstarter campaign, raising more than $112,000 toward a much-anticipated expansion. Chef Paulsen will be grateful for the additional kitchen space—the Birchwood puts out an astonishing amount of food from a tiny little kitchen—and the Seward neighborhood can relax knowing their Good Real Food gathering spot isn't going anywhere.

MAPLED BUTTERNUT SQUASH SOUP

(SERVES 6)

For the spiced pepitas (makes 1 cup):

1 cup pepitas (pumpkin seeds)
1 teaspoon olive oil
Dash of cayenne pepper
Dash of cinnamon
½ teaspoon salt, or more to taste

For the soup:

6 medium butternut squash
2 cups heavy cream
1 cup vegetable stock
2 teaspoons sambal or Sriracha
½ cup maple syrup
Kosher salt
Freshly ground black pepper

For the squash soup bowls:

6 butternut squash bottoms, seeded
2 tablespoons melted unsalted butter
Kosher salt
Freshly ground black pepper

For garnish:

Crispy bacon
Unsweetened yogurt or whipped cream
Spiced pepitas

To make the spiced pepitas: Preheat oven to 300°F. In a small mixing bowl, combine pepitas with oil, spices, and ½ teaspoon salt.

Spread pepitas evenly on a baking sheet and roast until seeds are golden and crackling, 10–15 minutes. Sprinkle with additional salt, if desired.

To make the soup: Preheat oven to 400°F. Line a baking sheet with parchment paper and brush or spray lightly with oil.

Slice squash crosswise, separating the hollow, seed-filled, bulbous base from the solid neck. Reserve the base portion for the soup bowls. Halve the top portions lengthwise and place flesh side down on the prepared baking sheet.

Roast squash until skins are scorched and flesh is soft, about 45 minutes (check progress at 30 minutes). Scoop flesh into the bowl of a blender and discard skins. (Note: While you prepare the rest of the soup, roast the squash-bottom bowls, below.)

Working in two batches, puree squash with cream, stock, sambal, and maple syrup. Transfer soup to a dutch oven or other large soup pot, season to taste with salt and pepper, and set aside while you finish the squash soup bowls.

To make the squash soup bowls: Preheat oven to 400°F. Line a baking sheet with parchment paper and brush or spray lightly with oil.

If necessary, trim the bottoms of the squash bowls a bit so they sit evenly on the baking sheet. Brush insides of bowls with melted butter and sprinkle lightly with salt and pepper.

Roast squash bowls until just tender and lightly golden brown, about 30 minutes; make sure they are not so soft that they won't hold their shape.

To serve: When ready to serve, heat soup over medium heat until steaming, season to taste with salt and pepper, and serve in squash bowls with garnishes.

BUTCHER & THE BOAR

1121 HENNEPIN AVENUE SOUTH
MINNEAPOLIS, MN 55403
(612) 238-8888
BUTCHERANDTHEBOAR.COM
EXECUTIVE CHEF/CO-OWNER: JACK RIEBEL
CO-OWNER: TIM ROONEY

I'm always amused to walk into Butcher & the Boar, and it's not just because Executive Chef Jack Riebel is one of the most gregarious people on the planet. There is just something so delightfully Minnesotan about the sight of a group of nightclub-bound young ladies, otherwise devoted to yoga, juicing, and quinoa, tossing back bourbon while platters of glistening, smoky meat are set before them. Their eyes sparkle like the sequins on their dresses as they devour meat-tastic specialties like the smoked beef long rib (one of the best dishes in all of Minneapolis–St. Paul), wild boar head cheese, and grilled Berkshire pork-and-cheddar sausage. Butcher & the Boar is a decidedly masculine place, and the ladies are in love with it.

As are the gents . . . and everyone. Butcher & the Boar was chosen a 2013 James Beard Award semifinalist for Best New Restaurant, and chef Jack Riebel was nominated as Best Chef Midwest. In late 2013 the *Wall Street Journal* listed the restaurant as one of the country's top twenty meateries. And local kudos abound as well: Named as the *Star Tribune*'s Best Restaurant of 2012 and recipient of The Charlie Awards (the Twin Cities' own food awards) 2013 Restaurant of the Year, Butcher & the Boar is slammed feeding diners and framing awards.

Some chefs might kick back and enjoy the accolades, but as Riebel says, "No one becomes a chef if they don't have a lot of energy. I have a lot of energy."

No kidding.

Riebel's the go-to chef for the Lake Minnetonka set's private fund-raising dinners not just because his food is stunning (it is), or because he's a well-oiled machine after stints in the best kitchens in Minneapolis–St. Paul (he is), but because he radiates enthusiasm and charm. Smart as a whip and funny, Riebel is a natural in front of a crowd, which means he's a regular on the TV demo circuit as well as local cooking competitions.

Like Riebel, the rest of the Butcher & the Boar team is on creative overdrive. Chef Peter Botcher, the talent behind the top-notch charcuterie and sausage offerings, has launched a line of sausages for sale at Lunds & Byerly's grocery stores. Co-owner Tim Rooney has overseen the addition of a beer garden and private event space. The whole team puts on a rotating series of events, including monthly beer bashes, an annual Boar Fest, and a first-ever Crawdad Fest in 2013.

But until then, you'll find Riebel running the deliciously smoke-filled kitchen at Butcher & the Boar. If you go, you must order the grilled oysters, anything pickled (vegetables, eggs, beef heart, all fantastic), of course the wild boar sausage, all of the comforting sides, a bourbon flight, and one (or more) of the superb beers. If you're lucky enough to be seated next to the wood-fired grill, you might wake up in the middle of the night noticing your hair smells like a bonfire. Sweet meaty dreams!

CHEF JACK'S JALAPEÑO POPPERS

(MAKES 30 POPPERS)

Note: Poppers, chipotle cream, and pico de gallo can all be made one day ahead; cover and refrigerate. Bring poppers to room temperature before baking.

For the chipotle cream (makes 1½ cups):

1 cup crème fraîche
6 dried chipotle peppers, soaked per package
   instructions, soaking liquid reserved, stems
   discarded, seeds removed from 3 of the peppers
½ tablespoon salt
1 lime, juiced

For the micro pico de gallo (makes 3½ cups):

3 cups ripe, finely diced tomatoes
3 jalapeños, seeded and diced finely
3 cloves garlic, minced
⅓ cup chopped coarsely cilantro
1½ limes, juiced
⅓ cup sliced scallions
3 tablespoons extra-virgin olive oil
Salt

For the poppers:

15 jalapeño peppers
1 pound fontina cheese (or your favorite melting cheese)
15 thin slices Serrano ham, cut in half lengthwise

For the garnish:

Chipotle cream
Micro pico de gallo
¼ pound cotija cheese, grated
Olive oil
Sprigs of fresh cilantro

To make the chipotle cream: Combine all of the ingredients except the chipotle-soaking water in the bowl of a blender. Blend on medium-high speed, drizzling in soaking liquid as necessary to reach a creamy, spoonable consistency.

To make the pico de gallo: Combine all of the ingredients (except salt) in a medium-size mixing bowl. Add salt to taste.

To make the poppers: Preheat oven to 375° F.

Fill a dutch oven or other large pot with water and bring to a boil over high heat. Fill a large bowl with ice water and set aside.

Meanwhile, wearing gloves to protect your skin from the peppers' oils, cut jalapeños in half lengthwise. Remove and discard seeds. Blanch peppers in boiling water for 1 minute, drain in a colander, then quickly transfer peppers into ice water bath. (Blanching reduces the heat of the peppers, while the ice-water bath maintains their crunch by halting the cooking.)

Cut the fontina cheese into approximately 1 x ⅜-inch pieces (or pieces that will fit snugly into the jalapeños, depending on their size). Nestle cheese into the halved jalapeños and wrap the peppers and cheese with thinly sliced Serrano ham.

Place wrapped jalapeños on a lightly oiled or parchment-lined baking sheet and bake them for 3–4 minutes, or until the cheese is melted and the ham is crispy. (Alternately, you can grill the poppers on a hot grill.)

To serve: Smear a dollop of the chipotle cream on a serving plate, then settle poppers on top of the cream. Spoon the pico de gallo over the poppers and top with cotija cheese, a drizzle of olive oil, and a few sprigs of fresh cilantro. Serve immediately.

THE BUTTERED TIN

237 7TH STREET EAST
ST. PAUL, MN 55101
(651) 224-2300
THEBUTTEREDTIN.COM
CO-OWNER: JENNIFER LUECK
CO-OWNER/PASTRY CHEF: ALICIA HINZE
CHEF: JASON SCHELLIN

Jennifer Lueck and Alicia Hinze had never met, but they shared a dream. Lueck was busy doing public relations for restaurants, while Hinze was dazzling Food Network viewers as she competed on—and won—*Cupcake Wars*. At night, the two would lay their heads on their respective pillows with visions of pastries and eggs served to happy families dancing in their heads. By the time the two actually met, the cozy-chic, buttery-walled cafe was all but planned, and the two set about bringing The Buttered Tin to life.

Grateful diners line up on weekends for the opportunity to feast on crispy loaded hash browns, sandwiches stuffed with house-roasted, thick-sliced meats draped in scratch-made gravy, farm-fresh eggs any way you like them, and of course buttery pastries of the gluten-full and gluten-free varieties. If you can't wait for a seat, take away a slice of rich banana bread studded with dark chocolate, a bag of their golden, toasty granola, or dark chocolate cupcakes filled with white pastry cream and glazed with chocolate ganache—reminiscent of a famous childhood treat, but way, way better.

The Buttered Tin's Lowertown St. Paul neighbors are still pinching themselves that the ladies' dream became their delectable reality.

HUEVOS RANCHEROS SAUCE

(MAKES 1 QUART)

The Buttered Tin serves their rancheros sauce with cornbread-topped poached eggs, avocado, roasted-corn and black-bean salsa, cilantro-lime sour cream, and crispy tortilla strips.

2 jalapeño peppers
2 tablespoons vegetable oil
1 medium yellow onion, chopped
4 cloves garlic, chopped
1 teaspoon chili powder
1 teaspoon ground cumin
2 teaspoons salt, plus more to taste
2 teaspoons black pepper
2 teaspoons dried oregano
1 quart whole tomatoes
2 cups chicken stock, plus more if necessary

Under a broiler or directly on a gas burner, char jalapeños until blackened in spots. Cool and trim away the stem. Chop pepper coarsely.

Set a large saucepan over medium heat and add the oil. When oil is hot, add onions and garlic and stir to coat with oil. Sauté until onions and garlic are lightly brown, about 15 minutes. Add chili powder and cumin and sauté until fragrant, about 3 minutes.

Add salt, pepper, oregano, jalapeños, tomatoes, and stock. Bring to a boil, then turn heat to low and simmer, uncovered, for 20 minutes. Puree in a blender or with a stick blender. Add more chicken stock as needed to achieve sauce consistency. Season with additional salt to taste.

GLUTEN-FREE CARROT CAKE

(SERVES 12)

Chef Hinze's note: You'll get the most consistent result by weighing the ingredients.

9 ounces (1⅘ cups) white rice flour

14 ounces (2 cups) sugar

1½ tablespoons cinnamon

¾ teaspoon baking soda

¼ teaspoon baking powder

½ teaspoon salt

4 large eggs

6 ounces (⅘ cup) vegetable oil

1 pound carrots, peeled and grated

2½ ounces chopped walnuts

Your favorite cream cheese icing

Preheat oven to 350°F. Lightly grease two 9-inch cake pans and line with parchment circles.

In a large mixing bowl, sift together the rice flour, sugar, cinnamon, baking soda, baking powder, and salt. Stir in the eggs and vegetable oil and mix until combined. Add in the carrots and the walnuts and stir until incorporated.

Divide batter equally between the two pans. Bake for 45–55 minutes or until tester comes out clean. Cool cakes completely on racks before removing from pans and frosting with cream cheese icing. Store leftover cake in the refrigerator.

CAFE BARBETTE

1600 W. LAKE STREET
MINNEAPOLIS, MN 55408
(612) 827-5710
BARBETTE.COM
OWNER: KIM BARTMANN
EXECUTIVE CHEF: SARAH MASTER

LOOKING FORWARD TO COOKING YOU MANY MORE DELICIOUS MEALS IN THE FUTURE! ♡ Chef Sarah Master

Since it opened in 2001, Cafe Barbette has become an integral part of hip Uptown Minneapolis, flourishing under the ownership of successful local restaurateur Kim Bartmann. With several other popular, sustainability-focused restaurants in her mini empire, it's bohemian, French-influenced Barbette that's garnering most of the attention of late, thanks to the rising national celebrity of Executive Chef Sarah Master. In 2013 she appeared on the reality cooking show *The Taste*, where she fed celebrity chefs Anthony Bourdain, Ludo Lefebvre, Nigella Lawson, and Marcus Samuelsson, lasting for several rounds before returning to feed us hungry Twin Citians. We allow our chefs to go make a name for themselves on the national stage, but we're very happy when they return home to their kitchens!

Master is Minnesota born and raised, but she spent several years living in New Orleans, and it shows in her Creole-influenced dishes. Imagine classically prepared French bistro classics with a kick and you'll understand why Barbette is packed for the mimosa-sipping, omelet-scarfing brunch crowd as well as couples snuggling in a sexy corner booth on a Friday night, sharing moules frites under soft, amber lights.

Beet Salad of Roasted Beets, Pickled Beet Stems, Beet Gastrique, Beet Leaves & Beet Togarashi Vinaigrette

(SERVES 4)

2 bunches baby red beets, washed thoroughly, leaves and stems intact
3 cups water, divided
½ cup balsamic vinegar
1½ cups sugar, divided
3 cups canola oil, divided
Kosher salt
⅓ cup plus ¼ cup rice vinegar
2 tablespoons plus ¼ cup soy sauce
2 teaspoons togarashi seasoning
2 teaspoons sambal oelek, divided
4 French breakfast radishes, trimmed and sliced thinly
2 cups arugula
2 oranges, peeled and cut into segments
Freshly ground black pepper

For the roasted beets and gastrique: Preheat oven to 400°F. Trim the stems and leaves from 8 beets, about 1 inch from the top of the beets, reserving the stems and leaves.

Put the beets, water, and balsamic vinegar in a small covered, oven-safe saucepan. Cover tightly and place in the oven. Cook for about 40 minutes or until a knife can be smoothly inserted into the beets. (Keep oven on.)

Using tongs, remove beets from the cooking liquid and transfer to a large plate. Add 1 cup sugar to the cooking liquid and set over medium heat. Bring to a boil, uncovered, and continue boiling until liquid is reduced by three-quarters and gastrique has become syrup-like in consistency. Remove from heat and set aside to cool.

Rub the skins off the warm beets. Discard the skins, cut the beets into quarters, and set them aside to cool completely.

For the beet chips: Add 2 cups of the canola oil to a small saucepan and heat to 350°F. While oil heats, trim and peel 2 of the beets, reserving stems, leaves, and peel. Using either a mandoline or sharp knife, slice the beets paper thin. When oil is hot, add beet slices to the oil and fry for approximately 2 minutes or until crispy. Using a slotted spoon, transfer beet chips to paper towels. Season with salt to taste.

For the beet togarashi vinaigrette: Spread the beet skins reserved from above evenly on a cookie sheet and place in 400°F oven. Toast for about 10 minutes, until dry, crispy, and curled a bit. Cool to room temperature, then grind skins to dust in a coffee grinder or mortar and pestle.

In a large jar or other covered container, mix the beet dust with ⅓ cup rice vinegar, 2 tablespoons soy sauce, 2 teaspoons togarashi seasoning, and 1 teaspoon sambal oelek, whisking in 1 cup canola oil at the end. The vinaigrette does not have to be emulsified, but should be stored in a container that can be shaken prior to serving.

For the pickled beet stems: Thinly slice enough beet stems to fill ½ cup.

In a small saucepan, combine ¼ cup soy sauce, ¼ cup rice vinegar, ½ cup sugar, 1 cup water, and 1 teaspoon sambal oelek. Set pan over medium heat, bring to a simmer, then turn off heat and stir

in sliced beet stems. Steep stems for 15 minutes. Drain the stems, discarding the liquid. (Sarah's note: This is my favorite part of this dish. I often make a larger batch and keep them in my fridge to snack on. They'll keep up to 2 weeks if stored in the pickling liquid.)

To finish the salad: Slice beet greens into ½-inch slices. Transfer to a large bowl and add radishes, arugula, oranges, roasted beets, pickled stems, and vinaigrette to taste. Sprinkle with a little salt and pepper and mix thoroughly, adjusting seasoning.

To serve: Drizzle a little beet gastrique on four salad plates. Divide the tossed salad atop the gastrique and garnish with beet chips.

CAFE LEVAIN

4762 CHICAGO AVENUE SOUTH
MINNEAPOLIS, MN 55407
(612) 823-7111
CAFELEVAIN.COM
OWNER: HARVEY MCLAIN
EXECUTIVE CHEF: ADAM VICKERMAN

Tucked in off a side street in a quiet part of South Minneapolis, Cafe Levain isn't always easy to find, until you spot its signature red door. The understated entrance suits Executive Chef Adam Vickerman's style, who has quietly and consistently run one of the best kitchens in Minneapolis for the last several years . . . and he's not even thirty years old. Vickerman is a chef's chef, feeding plenty of post-service colleagues, tired and starving for polished, rustic cooking.

No one in this town makes a better roast chicken than Vickerman: locally sourced, perfectly seasoned, with crisp skin that shatters into supple, juicy flesh. Like several chefs in town, Vickerman counts on Riverbend Farm polenta, grown and ground just outside the Twin Cities. Vickerman coaxes the polenta into a decadent, creamy porridge, sometimes paired with that chicken, sometimes with silky braised beef, and always with what has become one of his signature touches: perfectly cooked vegetables. Vegetarians delight at Levain as Vickerman has pushed to expand his repertoire of grains, legumes, and peak-season vegetables, often plucked from Levain's own garden.

The kitchen at Levain is wide open to the dining room; in fact you can see straight through to sister cafe Turtle Bread on the other side of the building. Vickerman and long-time sous chef Remle Colestock work the cooking-in-the-open setting to their advantage. "Being able to see and receive instant feedback in our open kitchen helps that exponentially; to be able to easily communicate with our guests allows us to not only receive instant gratification in our jobs but to also grow and cultivate relationships with our guests."

Mushroom Soup with Fall Fruit Compote

(SERVES 4)

For the stewed mushrooms:

2 tablespoons unsalted butter
¼ pound fresh mushrooms (oyster, shiitake, button)
1 shallot, peeled and thinly sliced
1 clove garlic, peeled and thinly sliced
½ lemon
½ cup heavy cream
Water, as needed
Salt and freshly ground pepper

For the fall fruit compote:

½ pound assorted dried fruits (raisins, golden raisins, cherries, apricots, and/or currants)
1 quart port wine
2 tablespoons sugar

For the mushroom soup:

1 pound fresh, wild (if possible) mushrooms, depending on the season (morel, oyster, chicken of the woods, hen of the woods, porcini, etc.)
2 yellow onions, peeled and roughly chopped
2 russet potatoes, peeled and roughly chopped
1 quart heavy cream
1 pound unsalted butter (4 sticks)
4 quarts water, plus more as needed
2 tablespoons picked fresh thyme leaves
½ head garlic, peeled and roughly chopped
Salt and freshly ground pepper

For serving:

Stewed mushrooms (see recipe)
Warm fall fruit compote (see recipe)
4 fresh figs, quartered
4 tablespoons crumbled truffle pecorino (or other hard, crumbly cheese)
4 teaspoons minced chives

To make the stewed mushrooms: In a 12-inch skillet over medium-high heat, melt butter. Cook butter until brown flecks start to appear—it will foam first, then bubble, then start to brown and smell nutty. Add mushrooms to the brown butter and sauté until nicely caramelized. Add the shallot and garlic and sauté until translucent, about 4 minutes.

Deglaze the pan with a generous squirt of lemon juice and stir in the cream. Turn heat to medium-low and simmer until cream is thick and mushrooms are very tender, adding water if needed to keep the mixture moist, about 10 minutes. Season to taste with salt and pepper.

To make the fall fruit compote: Combine ingredients in a large saucepan set over medium heat. When mixture simmers, stir occasionally, cooking until fruit is nicely glazed with a thick sauce, about 30 minutes.

To prepare the soup: In a large soup pot, combine wild mushrooms, onion, potatoes, cream, butter, water, thyme, and garlic. Set over medium-high heat and bring to a boil. Turn heat to low and simmer until potatoes are cooked through and falling apart, about 30 minutes.

Working in batches, carefully puree hot soup in the bowl of a blender (or use a stick blender), until soup is very smooth and velvety. Be aware that blending hot liquids requires extra care, so never overfill the container. Thin with a bit of water if needed. Season to taste with salt and pepper.

To serve: Divide stewed mushrooms, warm fruit compote, figs, crumbled cheese, and chives among four warm shallow bowls. Pour hot soup over garnishes.

For years Twin Cities diners bemoaned our lack of a street dining scene (except for the ten days of the Minnesota State Fair, when more than a million of us hit it *hard*). Granted our al fresco dining season is short, but as a result we are maniacal about eating outdoors as often as possible from May through October. When pent-up demand softened an overly strict health code, a new era in outdoor dining was born, ushered in by the ladies of Chef Shack. Lisa Carlson and Carrie Summer launched their first truck in 2009, with a passion for locally raised innovative sandwiches, tacos, salads, and their now-famous mini donuts dusted in fragrant, Indian-inspired spices. They set a high bar for delivering chef-driven, innovative food from a truck window, and soon other chefs joined the fun. Chef Shack now operates several trucks: Track them down at chefshack.org.

Chef Erica Strait launched Foxy Falafel (perhaps one of the best food business names ever) as a stand at Kingfield Farmers' Market, building a wide following with her bike-powered smoothie blender and authentic recipe for sprouted-chickpea falafels topped with zingy condiments and pickles; her beloved truck, Roxy, joined the downtown

Minneapolis lunch scene a couple of years later. Follow the foxiness at foxyfalafel.com.

Chefs Christina Nguyen and Birk Grudem of Hola Arepa introduced Minneapolitans to the tender-crispy Venezuelan flatbread sandwiches stuffed with a variety of all things good and delicious (black beans, slow-roasted pork, chimichurri chicken, cheese, fried eggs, slaws, salsas, and more). They draw a serious lunch crowd with their scratch-made, locally sourced eats, including a loyal following of gluten-free diners. So does Sushi Fix, run by gregarious (and hilarious) sushi chef Billy Tserenbat. I confess that at first I couldn't imagine sushi from a truck, but oh my heavens, Tserenbat has delivered in spades, earning fans of skeptics and serving some of the best sushi in town. Find Hola Arepa at holaarepa.com and Sushi Fix at sushifix.net.

If fried fish is more your style, then The Anchor Fish & Chips is your truck. Chef Luke Kyle has mastered the art of tender fish surrounded by shatteringly crisp batter, paired with equally tender-crisp chips (fries). Add freshly made and classic sides like curry dipping sauce, mushy peas, and beans for the whole heavenly Brit experience. Follow along at theanchorfishandchips.com.

Even food celebrity and local chef-made-good Andrew Zimmern has gotten in on the action. He launched AZ Canteen in 2012 at the Minnesota State Fair, serving a flavor-packed mix of items from goat burgers to crispy pork belly with green papaya salad to dulce de leche shaved ice with pound cake. Track down your *cabrito* at azcanteen.com.

AZ Canteen—and in fact all of the trucks mentioned above—are part of phase two of the food truck movement: parlaying a successful truck following into a brick-and-mortar business. Chef Shack now has two restaurants, one in Bay City, Wisconsin, the other in the Seward neighborhood of Minneapolis. Foxy Falafel has a cafe in St. Paul, Hola Arepa opened in the Kingfield neighborhood of Minneapolis, Sushi Fix is now a fixture in downtown Wayzata, The Anchor Fish & Chips feeds hungry Northeast Minneapolis diners, and AZ Canteen is at Target Field with plans for the new Vikings stadium and beyond.

Whew! What a transformation in a very short period of time. Downtown Twin Cities lunchgoers couldn't be more thrilled, and the excitement has carried over to the many summertime concerts, art fairs, private parties, and farmers' markets made even better with a variety of trucks to feed the revelers. For a full list of Twin Cities food trucks, visit the Minnesota Food Truck Association at mnfoodtruckassociation.org. And for a taste of street food at home, try your hand at one of the recipes below.

AZ CANTEEN

ANDREW ZIMMERN, CHEF/OWNER

ANDOUILLE, CRAB & OYSTER GUMBO

(SERVES 8)

½ cup all-purpose flour

½ cup vegetable oil

1 pound andouille sausage, sliced ¼ inch thick

3 celery ribs, cut into ½-inch dice

1 onion, cut into ½-inch dice

1 red bell pepper, cut into ½-inch dice

1 habanero chile, minced and most seeds discarded

3 garlic cloves, minced

½ pound okra, sliced ¼ inch thick

2 teaspoons dried thyme

1 bay leaf

3 tablespoons filé powder, divided

5 cups chicken stock

3 cups bottled clam juice

3 tablespoons Worcestershire sauce

3 large tomatoes, finely chopped

1 pound lump crabmeat, picked over

24 shucked oysters and their liquor

Salt

Freshly ground pepper

In a large pot, stir the flour and oil until smooth to make a roux. Cook over moderate heat, stirring often, until the roux turns a rich brown color, about 15 minutes. Add the andouille, celery, onion, bell pepper, habanero, garlic, okra, thyme, bay leaf, and half of the filé powder, and cook over moderate heat, stirring, until the onion is translucent. Add the stock, clam juice, Worcestershire, and tomatoes; bring to a boil. Reduce the heat to low and simmer for 1 hour, stirring.

Stir in the remaining filé powder and add the crab and oysters and their liquor. Season with salt and pepper and simmer gently for 1 minute to just cook the oysters.

Chef Shack

Lisa Carlson and Carrie Summers, Chefs/Owners

Sweet Potato & Black Bean Tacos

(SERVES 6–8)

½ medium head red cabbage, cored and shredded

3 cups organic apple cider vinegar

½ cup sugar

3 cups cold water

1 tablespoon each black peppercorns, mustard seeds, coriander seeds, fennel seeds, and star anise

2 cloves garlic, smashed

¼ cup peeled and grated fresh ginger

¼ cup diced red onion

2 large sweet potatoes, peeled

Olive oil

Salt and freshly ground black pepper

1 tablespoon unsalted butter

1 teaspoon freshly ground cumin, divided

4 cups canned organic black beans and their juices

1 cup small-diced white onion

1 tablespoon diced jalapeño

1 tablespoon hot sauce (like Cholula, Tapatillo, or locally made Lucky's), plus another dash for sauce

2 cups sour cream

2 tablespoons prepared organic mayonnaise

2 tablespoons prepared organic ketchup

Juice of 1 lime

Fresh corn or flour tortillas

Put cabbage in a colander and rinse with cold water. Set aside in a cool place to drain. In a large saucepan, combine vinegar, sugar, water, spices, garlic, ginger, and red onion to make the pickle brine. Set over medium-high heat and bring to a boil. Transfer cabbage to a large bowl and pour hot pickle brine over the cabbage. Cover and set in refrigerator to chill.

Preheat oven to 375°F. Rub sweet potatoes with olive oil. Place each sweet potato on a piece of foil and season with salt and pepper. Wrap each potato in the foil and roast until fork-tender, 45–60 minutes. Let sweet potatoes cool enough to handle, then mash with butter, ½ teaspoon cumin, and salt and pepper to taste. Keep warm.

While potatoes roast, place beans and their liquid in a large, heavy-bottomed saucepan. Set over medium-high heat and bring to a boil, then turn heat to low and simmer beans, uncovered, until very tender and liquid is absorbed, 25–30 minutes. Add onion, jalapeño, hot sauce, and remaining ½ teaspoon cumin and mash together with a potato masher. Season to taste with salt and pepper. Keep warm.

In a medium bowl, stir together sour cream, mayonnaise, ketchup, lime juice, and salt, pepper, and a dash of hot sauce to taste.

To assemble and serve the tacos: Warm tortillas in a hot oven, in the fireplace, or in a sauté pan over high heat until they're soft and browned in spots. Add a generous spoonful of sweet potato mixture, then beans, then cabbage, and top with sour cream sauce.

Foxy Falafel

Erica Strait, Chef/Owner

Hummus

(MAKES 6 CUPS)

2 cloves garlic

4 cups canned or freshly cooked chickpeas, drained

¼ cup tahini

½ cup lemon juice

¼ cup olive oil, plus more for drizzling on top

1½ tablespoons salt

Pinch of black pepper

¼–½ cup water

Warm pita bread, for serving

Add garlic to the bowl of a food processor and puree. Add chickpeas, tahini, lemon juice, olive oil, salt, and pepper. Puree, adding just enough water to achieve a smooth, fluffy texture.

Transfer hummus to a bowl and swirl with spoon. Drizzle olive oil over the top and serve with warm pita bread.

Hola Arepa

Christina Nguyen and Birk Grudem, Chefs/Owners

Vigorón

(SERVES 4)

Vigorón is a dish from Nicaragua that's both refreshing and hearty. It's made of cooked yucca, topped with lots of citrus and a salad of cabbage and pico de gallo. It's traditionally served on a banana leaf and garnished with delicious crispy fried chicharrón. On the food truck, they like to serve it with their slow-roasted pulled pork on top for a little extra meatiness and to add to the flavor punch.

Note: Frozen yucca, frozen banana leaves, and freshly cooked chicharrón can be found at specialty Latin grocery stores.

12 ounces cabbage, thinly shredded, divided
Salt and freshly ground black pepper
1 pound Roma tomatoes (about 4), diced
4 ounces red onion, diced
½ bunch cilantro, chopped
4 soft, juicy limes, juiced, divided
1 jalapeño, finely minced (optional)
1½ pounds yucca, frozen or fresh, peeled
3 ounces chicharrón (crispy fried pork rind), broken into about 16 pieces
4 banana leaf sheets, thawed

Optional garnish:

If you have carnitas-style pulled pork already cooked, add that between the cabbage and pico de gallo layers for even more porky goodness!

Place half of the shredded cabbage in a colander. Rinse the cabbage with water and then salt generously. Let sit for 5–7 minutes (or until slightly softened) before rinsing salt off thoroughly with water. Drain.

Mix tomatoes, red onion, cilantro, half of the lime juice, salt, and pepper to taste for the pico de gallo. Add jalapeño for extra spice, if desired.

Set a large pot of salted water over high heat and bring to a boil. Add fresh or frozen (not thawed) yucca to the water and cook until fork tender, about 15 minutes (perhaps a bit longer for frozen).

While yucca is cooking, wipe the banana leaves with a damp cloth to remove residue. Divide leaves among four serving bowls or plates.

Remove yucca from pot and place on a cutting board. Cut into 4-inch batons that are roughly 1 x 1-inch-thick wedges (making sure to remove the hard fiber from the center of the yucca if it's still in place). Divide yucca among the serving plates, on top of the banana leaves. Sprinkle with salt and drizzle half of remaining lime juice on top of yucca.

In a large bowl, mix remaining cabbage with drained salted cabbage and layer it on top of the yucca. Top the cabbage with pico de gallo and remaining lime juice. Garnish each dish with 4 pieces of chicharrón, tucking it slightly under yucca and into cabbage layers.

Corner Table

4257 Nicollet Avenue
Minneapolis, MN 55409
(612) 823-0011
cornertablerestaurant.com
Co-Owners: Nick and Chenny Rancone
Co-Owner/Executive Chef: Thomas Boemer

If I were to tally total hours spent in any Twin Cities restaurant, Corner Table would hold the top spot. I am hardly in the minority; since opening in 2004, Corner Table has earned a deeply loyal following for its consistent mix of seasonal ingredients, inspired craft cooking, and warm hospitality. Fans of gregarious founding chef Scott Pampuch were concerned they'd lost a farm-to-table gem when he sold the restaurant in 2011, but they needn't have worried. While it's no easy task to recast a restaurant so closely identified with its founder, new owners Nick and Chenny Rancone and Executive Chef Thomas Boemer have done it in fine style. The Rancones graciously run the front of the house as well as Corner Table's outstanding wine program, while Boemer puts his delicious spin on Corner Table's reputation for high-integrity, house-made ingredients and dishes.

Boemer's style is classical meets comfort, with precise technique honed in the kitchen of Alain Ducasse's Mix in Las Vegas by way of a Southern upbringing. You're just as likely to find *torchon* of duck confit as beef brisket with cheesy grits on Corner Table's seasonally driven menu. From house-made charcuterie to Corner Table's award-winning pork belly with chowchow, Boemer's skills as a butcher (and pastry chef) and his loving treatment of pork are earning him serious local street cred. Every time I drop in for a good chat, lovely wine, and (depending on the season) a dish of cassoulet or ethereal morel risotto (meat tends to steal the spotlight, but vegetable dishes are equally sophisticated), there are other chefs sitting and chatting with Rancone and Boemer, drinking locally brewed beer and talking shop. Says Boemer, "Our Twin Cities food scene is an incredibly diverse and supportive community where professionals compete and collaborate in the same breath. I've never imagined anything like it could exist."

From my perspective, as a diner and a cook, I appreciate Boemer's generosity in answering questions about seasoning and technique. As a father and husband, he appreciates the challenges of a busy home cook and believes restaurant strategies—like a well-stocked pantry and finishing a dish with a touch of acid to lift and brighten flavors—can help home cooks put fast, flavorful meals on the table. To that end, along with Corner Table's signature pheasant galantine, Boemer has also shared recipes for pickled mustard seeds and preserved lemons, which can individually be used to finish a wide variety of dishes, from roasts to sandwiches to salads to eggs.

PANCETTA-WRAPPED PHEASANT BREASTS WITH SWEET GARLIC SAUCE

(SERVES 4)

Note: The pheasant breasts can be prepared and poached one day ahead (wrap, chill, and crisp and roast before serving). The sweet garlic sauce can be prepared one day ahead (cover and chill).

For the sweet garlic sauce (makes about 1½ cups):

2 pheasant carcasses with skin (reserved from pheasants, below)

½ cup finely diced celery

½ cup finely diced onion

½ cup finely diced carrot

1 teaspoon vegetable oil

¼ cup red wine

2 ounces tomato paste

1 sachet (bay leaf, thyme, and 5 peppercorns tied in cheesecloth)

10 peeled garlic cloves

3 cups milk, divided

1 cup heavy cream

Salt

For the pheasant:

2 whole pheasants, butchered and boned, bones and trimmings reserved

¼ teaspoon pâté spice (quatre épices)

2 garlic cloves, grated on a zester/grater

Salt

1 large egg

⅓ cup heavy cream

6 (⅛-inch-thick) slices of pancetta (mild smoked bacon can be substituted)

To make the sauce: Preheat oven to 350°F.

Combine carcass and skin trimmings in a large, lightly oiled roasting pan and roast until caramelized (but not burned), 1–1½ hours, turning bones halfway through.

While bones are roasting, add mirepoix (celery, onion, and carrots) to a small bowl and toss with oil. Spread mirepoix on a baking sheet and roast in the oven, alongside the bones, until caramelized (but not burned), about 20 minutes, stirring halfway through.

Transfer both caramelized bones and mirepoix to a large stockpot. Use wine to deglaze both pans and scrape into the stockpot. Add the tomato paste and sachet to the pot, and then add cold water to just cover the bones. Bring stock to a simmer over medium heat, then turn heat to low, and simmer very gently, uncovered, for 4 hours. Do not stir, but occasionally skim away any scum that floats to the surface.

Strain stock through a cheesecloth-lined colander over a large bowl. Clean stockpot, then return stock to pot and bring to a simmer over medium heat. Turn heat to medium-low and simmer, reducing stock by half or to jus (sauce) consistency (clings to a spoon), skimming occasionally, 30–60 minutes. Set aside.

In a small saucepan, combine the garlic and 1 cup milk. Bring to a boil over medium heat, remove from heat, and strain garlic through a colander (discarding milk). Repeat two more times. Return the blanched garlic to the saucepan and add cream. Bring to a simmer over medium heat, turn heat to low, and simmer until cream is reduced by one-third. Add garlic-cream mixture to the bowl of a blender and puree with jus until very smooth. Strain through chinois. Season with salt to taste.

To prepare the pheasant: Set skin-on pheasant breasts aside (to be stuffed, below).

To make the mousseline (stuffing paté): Remove skin from meat (thigh, leg, and tenderloin; reserve skin for making sweet garlic sauce). Using a paring knife, scrape tendons from legs. Add 10 ounces meat to a food processor with paté spice, garlic, and a generous pinch of salt, and process until the meat forms a sticky and firm ball. Add the egg and continue processing until fully incorporated. Add cream and process until smooth.

Set a dutch oven or other large pot of water over low heat.

Place two 12 x 12-inch sheets of plastic wrap side-by-side on work surface. Arrange 3 slightly overlapping pieces of pancetta on each sheet, using the back of a chef's knife to smooth pieces flat. Center 1 breast, skin side down, on pancetta. Trim the thickest part of each breast to an even thickness, sprinkle breasts lightly with a bit of salt, then spread each breast with mousseline. Roll the pancetta and breast together into a pancetta-wrapped cylinder, then cover the cylinder tightly with plastic wrap. Twist the ends tightly (like a piece of candy). Set out two more

12 x 12-inch sheets of plastic and wrap pancetta-pheasant cylinders again in a second layer of plastic, again tightly twisting ends. Tie ends with kitchen twine to secure.

Adjust heat under pot of water so water temperature reaches 170°F. Add pheasant-breast cylinders to water and press a clean dish towel over them (and into the water) to keep cylinders submerged. Poach breasts for 30 minutes (they will not be completely cooked through). Remove breasts from water and, leaving cylinders wrapped in plastic, cool at room temperature for an hour.

To finish, preheat oven to 400°F. Unwrap breasts (discard plastic) and tie pancetta-breast rolls with kitchen twine in two spots to secure their shape. Heat butter in a 10-inch, oven-safe skillet over medium-high heat. When butter is hot, add breasts and sear until pancetta is lightly browned on all sides, 5–7 minutes. Transfer pan to oven and roast breasts until center reaches 160°F, 10–15 minutes. Transfer breasts to a cutting board and let rest for 10 minutes.

To serve: Remove kitchen twine. Slice breasts into 1-inch-thick slices. Serve with hot sweet garlic sauce.

PICKLED MUSTARD SEEDS

(MAKES 3 CUPS)

1½ cups white wine vinegar
1½ cups water
½ cup sugar
½ teaspoon kosher salt
1 cup yellow mustard seeds

Combine all ingredients except mustard seeds in a large saucepan and bring to a simmer over medium heat. Stir in mustard seeds, turn heat to low, and cook until seeds are tender and bitterness has subsided, about 20 minutes.

Cool mixture to room temperature, then spoon into jars. Cover and refrigerate for up to two months.

PRESERVED LEMONS

(MAKES 1 QUART)

8 lemons (or depending on size of lemons, enough to fill
   each jar halfway)
1 box kosher salt
2 (1-quart) mason jars

Halve lemons lengthwise and place in large mixing bowl. Add enough salt to cover and mix by hand until lemons are covered in salt. Pack lemons into jars, filling gaps with additional salt where needed, until jars are half filled (leaving room for stirring as the lemons cure). Cover jars and set lemons aside on the counter.

Stir lemons twice a week for six weeks. When the skin of the lemon is leathery and the salt has turned into half salt, half bright lemon juice, the lemons are done.

FIKA

2600 PARK AVENUE
MINNEAPOLIS, MN 55407
(612) 871-4907
ASIMN.ORG
OWNER: AMERICAN SWEDISH INSTITUTE
EXECUTIVE CHEF: DUSTIN THOMPSON

Walking into the elegant, austere American Swedish Institute, with gleaming white walls and a large window affording a stunning view of the expansive lawn and historic Turnblad mansion, a visitor would likely expect contemporary art installations, grand event space, and a clever museum gift shop—but perhaps not a museum cafe serving some of the loveliest food in the Twin Cities. However, the cafeteria-style space—which expands onto that beautiful lawn in summer months—surprises and delights visitors with chef-driven, scratch-made Scandinavian small plates and pastries. Suffice it to say, this is definitely not Ikea food. In fact, the accolades are rolling in for Chef Thompson's creations: Named Best Lunch 2014 by the *Star Tribune* and America's Best Sandwiches 2013 by *Travel + Leisure* magazine, FIKA is fast becoming one of Minneapolis–St. Paul's favorite lunch spots.

Thompson comes to Nordic cuisine pretty naturally. "I grew up in a family with very strong Nordic roots. My grandparents were farmers, and they taught me to love the simplicity of cabbage, the resourcefulness of charcuterie, like head cheese—using the whole beast—and the warmth and nostalgia of keeping tradition. I love the idea of utilizing what is around you and translating the growing season into a yearlong culinary adventure through pickling, potting, and preservation. It's not based on scarcity necessarily, although many of our Midwestern Scandinavian traditions are seen through the lens of the Great Depression; it's more about pragmatism. Scandinavians are a very practical bunch."

Treat yourself and a dear friend to a dose of delicious Scandinavian practicality by planning a summer afternoon lunch on the patio—including wine, of course—and share several small plates of *smorgasar* (open-face sandwiches), salads, tender meatballs, dumplings, and cardamom bread pudding for dessert. Then stroll through the mansion's art exhibits, plan your next party—because the event spaces are incredible, and it goes without saying that the catering is top-notch—and shop on your way out the door. Summer perfection, right there, Minnesota style.

GRAVLAX

(SERVES 10)

¼ cup juniper berries

2 tablespoons whole black peppercorns

1 tablespoon fennel seeds

3 pounds kosher salt

3 pounds sugar

5 fresh bay leaves, pulverized

1 tablespoon dill seeds

Zest of 6 lemons

½ cup aquavit (North Shore brand preferred)

½ cup gin (North Shore brand preferred)

1 side (about 3½ pounds) sustainably farmed Scottish salmon, skin on, pin bones removed by fishmonger

1 pound fresh dill

Garnishes:

Mustard

Pickles

Fresh dill

Bread

Crackers

Mayonnaise

In a small skillet over low heat, toast the juniper berries and black peppercorns until fragrant. Remove from heat, cool, and grind coarsely in a coffee grinder or by hand with a mortar and pestle. Transfer to a large mixing bowl.

In same skillet over low heat, toast fennel seeds until fragrant. Cool and add to juniper berry mixture.

Add the rest of the ingredients—except salmon and dill—to the toasted spice mixture and mix thoroughly.

Lay a sheet of plastic wrap on kitchen counter or table to wrap the salmon securely from all sides; make sure it is large enough. Spread half of the spice mixture on the plastic, then top with half of the fresh dill. Nestle salmon, skin side down, over the cure mix, then spread the remaining spices over the flesh; top with remaining dill.

Tightly wrap the plastic wrap over the fish, then double-wrap the fish securely in a large sheet of aluminum foil. (The goal is to trap the liquid that will leach from the fish as it cures, so be generous with both the plastic and foil wrapping.)

Place the salmon on a baking sheet set on the bottom shelf of refrigerator, top with another baking sheet, and place something atop the sheet to weigh it down, such as a bag of sugar or a box of salt.

After 2 full days, unwrap salmon and rinse it well, patting dry with paper towels. Lay it flat on a baking sheet and place back in the refrigerator, uncovered, for at least 8 hours and up to 2 days, allowing the salmon to dry and cure evenly.

To finish, skin the gravlax and split the side lengthwise down the middle, following the line that divides the thick meaty loin from the thinner belly. Turn the gravlax over and carefully trim away any dark flesh (it will taste strong and fishy).

To serve, slice the gravlax against the grain as thinly as possible. Serve with mustard, pickles, fresh dill, bread, and crackers. Alternatively, chop the gravlax into small pieces, mix with mustard and mayonnaise, and serve as tartare-style dish. Gravlax can be stored in the refrigerator, wrapped in plastic, for up to a week.

FOREPAUGH'S RESTAURANT

276 S. EXCHANGE STREET
ST. PAUL, MN 55102
(651) 224-5606
FOREPAUGHS.COM
OWNER: BRUCE TAHER
EXECUTIVE CHEF: DONALD GONZALEZ

There's a stately Victorian home with a sweeping balcony in a historic part of St. Paul, just at the edge of downtown. Joseph Forepaugh's haunted (really!) mansion has endured many a change over the last 130 years, from family home to rooming house to restaurant, but there is no better time to dine there than right now. Under the supervision of Executive Chef Donald Gonzalez, who sources local, farm-fresh ingredients whenever possible, the inventive dishes are a stunning array of edible art and layers of big flavors. From traditional dishes like chicken gribeche (sauce gribeche, Spanish capers, olives, fingerling potatoes, seasonal greens, fresh radish) to decadent fusion compositions like wok-fried black pepper–glazed scallops (with pork belly, seasonal fruit, radish, agave jam, salsify chips, emerald celery, chervil), Gonzalez's seasonal cooking is exactly what

you would expect from a chef who has worked with some of the best-known names in the business, including chefs Thomas Keller and Jean-Georges Vongerichten—solid, classic technique infused with fresh, bright flavors.

So, back to this haunted rave. Not one but two ghosts are said to haunt the lovingly restored home— Mr. Forepaugh's himself and his tragic lover, Molly

the housemaid. Both are reported to be friendly ghosts who enjoy weddings and spiffy parties in particular, which means they must be happy ghosts indeed because the mansion is a stunning setting for any get-together, at once grand cozy, with period light fixtures, multiple fireplaces, views of beautiful Irvine Park, and one of the most romantic patios in the Twin Cities. But don't just wait for a balmy summer evening for dinner— the beautiful bar is a warm and inviting place to spend a cold winter's night, sipping Champagne and sharing elegant bar snacks like beef marrow with bacon-wrapped shrimp and foie gras poutine, as well as classic salads. And brunch is a family must-do in any of the sunny dining rooms. I don't know if there's a list somewhere of the Twin Cities' best restaurants to propose to someone, but if there were, Forepaugh's should be at the top.

DONALD'S DUCK

(SERVES 4 AS AN APPETIZER)

Note: Begin recipe the night before you plan to serve it.

For the duck confit:

½ cup kosher salt
1 teaspoon chopped fresh tarragon leaves
1 tablespoon chopped fresh cilantro leaves
2 teaspoons minced garlic
2 teaspoons minced Fresno chile
½ teaspoon minced, peeled fresh ginger
1 tablespoon seeded and crushed dried Guajillo chile
   (crushed into flakes with a mortar and pestle)
¼ teaspoon ground coriander
¼ teaspoon ground cumin
2 fresh skin-on, bone-in duck legs
Canola oil

For the pickled chiles and shallots:

1 Fresno chile, sliced ⅛ inch thick
1 large shallot, sliced ⅛ inch thick
½ cup apple cider vinegar

For the blackening spice:

3 tablespoons seeded and crushed dried Guajillo chiles
   (crushed into flakes with a mortar and pestle)
1 teaspoon cayenne pepper
1 teaspoon ground turmeric
1 teaspoon sugar
1 teaspoon salt

For the chile lime glaze:

¼ cup canola oil
3 tablespoons minced, peeled fresh ginger
½ cup chopped Fresno chile
½ cup sugar
¼ cup honey, plus more to taste if desired
½ cup fresh lime juice, plus more to taste if desired

For the rice tots:

⅓ cup heavy cream
⅓ cup Port Salut cheese
½ cup cooked basmati rice
3 tablespoons finely diced red onion

For the cilantro balls:

3 bunches fresh cilantro, washed and spun dry in a
   salad spinner
1 teaspoon ground coriander
1 teaspoon canola oil
2 teaspoons fresh lime juice
Kosher salt

For the fresh mango glaze:

1 ripe mango, peeled and pitted
½ tablespoon honey

For the duck breast:

1 fresh skin-on duck breast
Blackening spice

To finish and to serve:

Canola oil for frying rice tots
Cilantro balls (see recipe)
Pickled chiles and shallots (see recipe)
Chile-lime glaze (see recipe)
Fresh mango glaze (see recipe)

To make the confit: In a large bowl, toss together all ingredients except the duck legs and canola oil. Rub mixture generously onto duck legs, cover, and chill legs overnight (at least 12 hours).

Preheat oven to 225°F. Rinse duck legs and pat dry with paper towels. Place duck legs in a small, deep roasting pan or oven-safe pot and cover completely with canola oil.

On the stovetop over medium heat, heat the oil to 200°F. Transfer duck to the oven and cook for 2 hours, or until a wooden pick easily pierces the meat all the way to the bone. Remove duck from oven and cool in the oil until you can handle the duck legs without burning yourself. Remove the skin and the meat (which should be falling off the bone). Drain away any fat from the meat and chop meat into small dice.

For the chiles and shallots: Combine chile and shallot in a small bowl. Add apple cider vinegar, cover, and store in the refrigerator overnight.

To make blackening spice: In a small bowl, mix ingredients thoroughly.

To make the glaze: In a medium saucepan over medium-high heat, heat oil to 325°F. Add ginger and cook until golden brown, about 4 minutes. Add remaining ingredients and bring to a boil. Reduce liquid to consistency of syrup, about 5 minutes.

Transfer syrup to a blender and puree on high speed for 3–5 minutes, until smooth. Reheat and strain through fine-mesh strainer. Adjust seasoning with honey and/or lime juice to taste.

To make the rice tots: In a small saucepan over medium heat, warm cream and cheese together until cheese is melted. Fold in rice and red onion.

Roll rice mixture into twenty 1½-ounce balls. Set aside.

To make cilantro balls: Cut off the cilantro stems below the first leaves and discard stems. Chop remaining cilantro into ½-inch pieces. In a medium bowl, toss the cilantro with coriander.

Add oil to a 12-inch skillet over medium heat. When oil is hot, sauté cilantro until it begins to wilt and turns bright green. Add the lime juice, toss, and remove from heat. Add salt to taste. Spread mixture on paper towels to drain and place in the refrigerator to cool for about 15 minutes.

Once cooled, in a medium-size bowl, fold together 2 parts cilantro and 1 part diced duck confit. Form into balls the same size as the rice tots. Heat in a 12-inch skillet over low heat to warm.

To make the fresh mango glaze: Place the mango and honey in the bowl of a blender and blend for 3 minutes. Strain through a fine-mesh strainer.

To prepare the duck: Preheat oven to 400°F. Pat dry the skin side of the breast with paper towels. Spread the blackening spice on a flat surface and press the skin side of the duck into the spice mix; the entire skin should coated.

Heat a 10-inch skillet over high heat until almost smoking and press the skin side of the breast firmly into the hot pan. Sear duck until spice is charred, then transfer pan to oven and roast duck breast until the internal temperature of the breast is 110°F, about 10 minutes. Set aside to rest.

To finish: In a large saucepan over medium-high heat, heat 2 inches of oil to 350°F. Fry rice tots in batches until evenly golden brown, transferring to a paper-towel-lined baking sheet as they finish.

To serve: Arrange hot rice tots and warm cilantro balls across a large plate. Slice duck breast and transfer to plate. Arrange pickled chiles and shallots around the plate. Spoon chile-lime glaze and fresh mango glaze in spots around plate. Serve immediately.

FRENCH MEADOW BAKERY & CAFE/ BLUESTEM WINE BAR

2610 LYNDALE AVENUE SOUTH
MINNEAPOLIS, MN 55408
(612) 870-7588
FRENCHMEADOWCAFE.COM
FOUNDER/CO-OWNER: LYNN GORDON
CO-OWNER: STEVE SHAPIRO
EXECUTIVE CHEF: GEORGE LOHR

The first certified organic bakery in the United States, French Meadow Bakery & Cafe has long led the way for Minnesota-style delectable dining with a conscience. The operation has evolved several times since first opening in 1985, including a recent facelift and expansion at the flagship Uptown Minneapolis location. Chic Bluestem Wine Bar now links to the original cozy cafe, with expanded space for private dinners and wine tastings. In addition to French Meadow counters at Minneapolis–St. Paul International Airport and the Minnesota State Fair, a brand-new French Meadow Bakery & Cafe opened in St. Paul on Grand Avenue in March 2014.

With a focus on good food for everyone, founder Lynn Gordon made French Meadow a hot spot for vegetarian, vegan, organic, farm-to-table, and gluten-free dining years before any of those options were trendy. Whether eating in the restaurant, sipping at the wine bar, snacking on the sunny patio, or stocking up at the decadent-meets-healthy pastry case, French Meadow is one-stop shopping for diners of all ages and preferences. On weekends in particular, fans flock from cities and suburbs to

savor their famous breakfasts, which include a breakfast burrito the size of your arm as well as heavenly french toast accented with orange zest and drizzled with local maple syrup. Throughout the day and into evening, guests linger over glasses of biodynamic wines and Executive Chef Lohr's comforting dishes, like locally raised chicken and gluten-free waffles, and grass-fed steak frites.

Low Country Shrimp & Cheese Grits with Redeye Gravy

(SERVES 4 GENEROUSLY)

For the cheese grits:

3 cups free-range chicken stock

3 cups grass-fed whole cow's milk

1 cup stone-ground organic cornmeal

3 cups shredded sharp cheddar cheese

Salt and freshly ground pepper

For the redeye gravy:

1 medium yellow onion, peeled, trimmed, and halved

1 (15-ounce) can organic tomato sauce

1½ cups brewed coffee

⅓ cup favorite hot sauce (Franks, Crystal, Texas Pete's, etc.)

¼ cup Worcestershire sauce

1 bay leaf

Salt and freshly ground pepper

For the shrimp and to serve:

2 tablespoons vegetable oil

1 pound large shrimp (preferably Gulf or Carolina), peeled and deveined, patted dry with paper towels

Salt and freshly ground pepper

1 pound andouille sausage, halved lengthwise and sliced crosswise into ¼-inch slices

1 red bell pepper, diced small

1 green bell pepper, diced small

4 stalks celery, diced small

1 medium onion, peeled and diced small

1 bunch scallions, sliced ¼ inch thick, 2 tablespoons reserved for garnish

To make the cheese grits: Fill the bottom half of a double boiler with enough water to touch the bottom of the top pot when the two are assembled. Place water over high heat. When water boils, turn heat to low so water gently simmers. Set top pot over boiling water and add chicken stock and milk. When the mixture is steamy, slowly whisk in cornmeal. Cook grits, uncovered, for 45 minutes, stirring periodically. Grits are done when they start to pull away from the sides of the pan and are thick and tender.

Stir cheddar cheese into hot grits until melted. Season to taste with salt and pepper. Keep warm.

To make the redeye gravy: Brûlée (or scorch) the halved onion in a small skillet over medium-high heat until dark brown all over.

Combine tomato sauce, coffee, hot sauce, Worcestershire sauce, bay leaf, and brûléed onion in a large saucepan set over medium heat. When gravy simmers, turn heat to medium-low and reduce sauce to nape (sauce coats the back of a spoon).

Strain sauce through a colander, discarding solids, and season to taste with salt and pepper. Keep warm.

To make the shrimp: Set a 12-inch skillet over medium-high heat. Add vegetable oil and, when oil shimmers, add the shrimp. Season shrimp lightly with salt and pepper while in pan. Shrimp cook quickly, so when they start to turn pink, after about 2 minutes, stir andouille sausage, peppers, celery, diced onion, and scallions into the pan. Sauté for 4–5 minutes, until vegetables are just softening and releasing juices into the pan. Stir in the redeye gravy and continue cooking until shrimp are just cooked through, 2–3 minutes. Remove from heat.

To serve: Divide grits among four warm bowls. Spoon shrimp and redeye-gravy mixture over grits. Garnish with reserved scallions. Enjoy!

Gardens of Salonica

19 5th Street Northeast
Minneapolis, MN 55413
(612) 378-0611
GARDENSOFSALONICA.COM
Executive Chef/Co-Owner: Anna Christoforides
Co-Owner: Lazaros Christoforides

Food fans in the know have long named Gardens of Salonica as the best Greek restaurant in the Twin Cities. From classic mezes like *skordalia* and *tarama*, to flaky-savory *bougatsa* pastries, to well-loved entrees like *moussaka*, Gardens is a favorite spot to enjoy lunch or an after-work bite and glass of wine. But not everyone realizes that Executive Chef Christoforides has been sourcing and promoting locally raised, sustainably sourced ingredients since she and her husband, Lazaros, opened in 1991. Christoforides shares her passion for best-quality ingredients and Greek food and culture in her restaurant as well as by teaching classes, catering events, speaking about locally sourced food, and guiding groups on tours of Greece.

The day I photographed Christoforides, it was brutally, horribly cold outside. Very Minnesota. What a pleasure to sit in Gardens of Salonica's cheerful dining room, soaking in the sun and sipping hot tea while Greek music played softly in the background. We talked about food, of course, and photography (Christoforides is a photographer herself), and she pointed out the pieces of art that attract customers the most (both dining rooms

display striking sculptures). The scent of freshly baked bread was in the air, and the space made me feel like I was in Greece, which is exactly the effect Christoforides hopes for. "As an art student with four children post grad, I recognized that well-made food engages all the senses: sight, sound, taste, touch, and the most enduring memory, smell. My focus and goal was only and ever to make food that delights all the senses and invigorates both body and spirit."

I'm quite sure her many loyal customers would agree: She has succeeded.

ARNI FRICASEE

LAMB SHANKS WITH GREENS IN LEMON SAUCE

(SERVES 6)

6 (12- to 16-ounce) lamb shanks

1 cup extra-virgin olive oil

4 cups dry white wine

Salt and freshly ground pepper

3 medium heads of romaine lettuce, sliced crosswise into ½-inch pieces

3 bunches of scallions, sliced into ½-inch pieces

6 large eggs, lightly beaten

2 cups freshly squeezed lemon juice

Set a large dutch oven or other large, covered pot that snugly accommodates the lamb shanks over medium-high heat and add ¼ cup of the olive oil. When oil is hot, brown shanks on all sides. Drizzle the remaining oil over the shanks, pour in the wine, and season shanks with salt and pepper. When liquid is simmering, turn heat to low, cover pan, and braise shanks, turning every half hour or so, until very tender and nearly falling off the bone, 3–4 hours. Using tongs, remove shanks to a large platter, tent with foil to keep warm, and set aside.

Add the lettuce and scallions to the pan juices and cover the pan for a few minutes so greens wilt and can be stirred into the juices. Simmer uncovered until greens are tender-crisp, about 10 minutes. Turn off heat and allow greens to cool slightly.

While the greens cool, prepare the lemon sauce by beating the eggs in a bowl large enough to accommodate more than twice their volume. Slowly beat the lemon juice into the eggs until incorporated.

While whisking the egg-lemon mixture, slowly pour a ladleful of the hot pan juices into the eggs to temper them. Continue whisking while adding several more ladlefuls of pan juices. Return the shanks to the pan, nestling them among the greens, then slowly pour the tempered egg-lemon sauce over the shanks and greens. Gently swirl the pan to mix the egg-lemon sauce among the greens and shanks. The egg-lemon sauce should thicken from the heat of shanks and greens. If not, turn on heat to lowest setting and reheat until sauce is steaming, but not boiling.

Serve hot in warm shallow bowls.

THE GRAY HOUSE

610 W. LAKE STREET
MINNEAPOLIS, MN 55408
(612) 823-4338
THEGRAYHOUSEEATS.COM
OWNER/EXECUTIVE CHEF: IAN GRAY

Great nicknames are earned, and there is good reason that Chef Ian Gray is now known as the goat guy. Gray and Singing Hills Goat Dairy have formed a beautiful, delicious friendship, with Gray incorporating Singing Hills' award-winning chèvre and luscious goat meat into a variety of dishes. From goat livers dusted with ginger and seared with onions and fennel to garlicky goat meatballs served with kale and *skyr* (a yogurt-like cheese), Gray is winning converts to mild, tender goat meat.

There are plenty of other dishes to try, too, with a seasonally changing menu chock-full of fresh-from-the-farm produce, big flavors, and Gray's silky house-made pastas. A large chalkboard hangs on one wall—gray of course—with a long list of the current menu's farms. Everything is made from scratch, including the bread plate, which is exactly what Gray hoped for when he thought about what The Gray House could be. "Things can always change, especially when you work with the freshest local products available. Weather changes growth and availability, seasons bring new product, market dictates quantity and price. But since I opened my own place, I get to make all the decisions, which is tough at times, but it fulfills the sense of accomplishment I've desired."

The Gray House is Gray's first solo venture, after stints cooking at Trattoria Tosca and Cafe Lurcat. His goal in setting out on his own, and establishing himself in the Lynn-Lake neighborhood of Minneapolis, was to serve terrific beer with farm-fresh, creatively prepared food in a relaxed, convivial atmosphere. In fact, the definition of the word *gastropub* is printed on The Gray House website to set the tone. Despite his young age, he's achieved it all.

Goat Burgers

(MAKES FOUR 8-OUNCE BURGERS)

Chef Gray's serving suggestion: pickles, a salad, roasted vegetables, or . . . french fries. And a great beer!

2 pounds ground goat meat (Singing Hills Goat Dairy preferred)

4 ounces chèvre goat cheese (Singing Hills Goat Dairy preferred)

⅓ cup minced fresh chives

¼ cup minced fresh parsley

1 tablespoon fresh oregano leaves

2 tablespoons salt

1 tablespoons black pepper

1 tablespoons red pepper flakes

½ cup high-heat cooking oil (such as safflower, peanut, or canola oil

1 cup goats curd (Singing Hills Goat Dairy preferred)

4 brioche buns, halved and toasted

1 bunch lacinato kale, center ribs removed, roughly chopped

In a large bowl, combine goat meat, chèvre, chives, parsley, oregano, salt, pepper, and red pepper flakes. Mix thoroughly with your hands and form into four equal burgers.

Preheat oven to 425°F. Heat a 12-inch oven-safe sauté pan over medium-high heat and add oil. Tilt the pan a bit to coat the bottom of the pan evenly, and when oil is hot, add the patties. Cook until nicely browned with a good crust, 4–5 minutes, then turn burgers with a spatula and transfer pan to the oven. Roast burgers 3–4 minutes, then open the oven door and add curds to the pan around the burgers. Roast for another 3–4 minutes.

Meanwhile, set out toasted buns. Remove pan from oven, transfer the burgers to the buns, and add kale to the pan. Mix the cheese and kale until the kale is wilted, over medium heat if necessary, then divide kale-cheese mixture among the burgers.

First-time visitors to Minneapolis are always a bit in awe of our skyway system, which connects fifty-two blocks (nearly five miles) of downtown, making it possible to live, eat, work, and shop without going outside. That's a wonderful thing when it's −20°F, but after spending several months primarily indoors, deprived of daylight, Minnesotans flood outdoors like water over Minnehaha Falls when spring arrives, ready to bike, hike, golf, eat on patios, and shop for fresh food all summer long. It's no mystery why farmers' markets are so wildly popular and becoming more so every year: They are the antidote to long Minnesota winters, and when the season opens, we are ready to bust some market moves.

And not just by shopping for vegetables! Not that just-picked, fresh-from-the-farm vegetables aren't fun—there is something so joyful about spotting the season's first asparagus, ramps, and morel mushrooms. And picking up grass-fed beef and spring onions to grill on the season's first warm night? Heavenly. But the experience of just being at the market is awfully fun, too. There's no better spot to nibble a gooey caramel roll or a smoky bratwurst while watching a cooking demo than at the Minneapolis Farmers' Market, Minnesota's largest. The St. Paul Farmers' Market is the oldest in the state and is a particularly wonderful place to talk in depth with farmers and specialty-food purveyors about how they grow and prepare their food. Also in St. Paul, Hmongtown Marketplace is an incredible indoor/outdoor marketplace with more than two hundred stalls featuring flavors and prepared dishes of Southeast Asia. Several city neighborhood markets have popped up in the last few years, allowing the food trucks to get in on the action, as well as favorite bakeries, coffee roasters, musicians, smaller farms, and more. As a bonus, I always run into someone I know, no matter which market I choose, just in time for good tips on items I might have missed or ideas for preparing the bounty when I get home. If I'm lucky, I'll swipe a few fried cheese curds and a sip of a kombucha from a generous friend. For a comprehensive list of Minnesota farmers' markets, see Minnesota Grown at minnesotagrown.com.

And when the season ends? Twin Citians head to Midtown Global Market, an internationally themed indoor public market with more than fifty vendors who deliver color and flavor in doses fully capable of curing the winter blues. There is nothing but good times to be found at Kitchen in the Market, a shared commercial kitchen space and culinary school

known for their innovative, interactive, and entertaining cooking classes. Spend an evening cooking with a favorite local chef, singing karaoke while cooking with friends, or tasting wine with some of the top sommeliers in town. Classes make use of the locally sourced produce, pastured meats, farm-fresh eggs, and some of the best cheeses in the country found at Grassroots Gourmet and Produce Exchange. In addition, the nationally acclaimed and beloved Salty Tart bakery makes its home at Midtown Global, as do fast-casual favorites Manny's Tortas, Sonora Grill, and La Loma Tamales. Holy Land Grocery, Butcher Shop & Deli, and El Burrito Mercado offer Middle Eastern and Mexican specialty ingredients and take-out deli items. And in 2013, The Rabbit Hole brought much-needed craft cocktails—and killer Korean-fusion dishes—to the mix, making it possible to spend an afternoon shopping and sharing snacks and an evening enjoying a lovely, sit-down dinner. See Midtown Global Market's website at midtownglobalmarket.org for a listing of vendors and events.

Kitchen in the Market and Tastebud Catering

Molly Hermann, Executive Chef

Ground-Cherry Chutney

(MAKES ABOUT 1 CUP)

3 cups ground-cherries, husked and rinsed

30 dried apricots, quartered

1½ cups organic sugar

⅔ cup dried cherries

4 tablespoons peeled and minced fresh ginger

4 tablespoons orange juice

1½ teaspoons cinnamon

½ teaspoon cayenne pepper

Combine all ingredients in a medium saucepan. Set over medium heat and stir to dissolve sugar. Turn heat to high, bring to a boil, and boil for 3 minutes.

Transfer chutney to a bowl and cool to room temperature. Serve or store in an airtight container in the refrigerator for up to 2 weeks.

HauteDish

119 Washington Avenue North
Minneapolis, MN 55401
(612) 338-8484
haute-dish.com
Co-Owner/Executive Chef: Landon Schoenefeld

Executive Chef Landon Schoenefeld grew up eating hotdish—a simple casserole in Minnesota speak, if you're not from 'round these parts—which gave him a taste for comfort food. While that's probably true for most local chefs, it was Schoenefeld who had the terrific idea to embrace his Tater-Tot roots and polish them with top-notch technique and best-quality ingredients. The play on words that makes up the restaurant's name—it's pronounced as "hotdish," his mother's idea—sums up what HauteDish is all about: Midwestern comfort food, elevated. In fact, of all Twin Cities' restaurants, HauteDish might best represent a true, modern Minnesota cuisine.

What does that mean? Take creamed peas on toast, a dish that, when I was a kid, meant a can each of cream of mushroom soup and tuna. Schoenefeld's version is one of the most popular on the menu, thick with real cream, smoked whitefish, and pecorino, topped with pickled shallots for zing. Fantastic. Ditto the meatloaf in a can—opened tableside because it's fun—with beefy mushroom gravy, roasted vegetables, creamy mashed potatoes, and tomato marmalade. And what about the hotdish? It's legendary,

with house-made Tater Tots as light as potato-puff clouds atop all the decadence you expect from the real deal. I suggest you read through the whole menu; you'll smile nostalgically while you get really, really hungry.

It's Schoenefeld's culinary talent and sense of humor that keep it all in check. HauteDish knows its North Loop demographic and meets it at the door with menu items asterisked with "It can be made gluten-free, baby!" where possible, an award-winning burger, an impressive local beer selection, and one of the best brunches in town. (P.S. Go on Saturday when there isn't a line.)

Mushroom Roll Stuffed with Crab & Gruyère

(SERVES 4 AS AN APPETIZER)

For the mushroom roll:

3 portobello mushroom caps, peeled, sliced ¼ inch thick

¼ cup melted duck fat (ask your butcher or specialty food store, or order online)

3 teaspoons fresh thyme leaves

Salt and freshly ground black pepper

½ cup king crab meat

2 tablespoons mayonnaise, or more if necessary

½ cup grated gruyère cheese

For the tomato marinade:

4 medium-size ripe tomatoes, roughly chopped

1 teaspoon salt, or more to taste

1 teaspoon sugar, or more to taste

2 tablespoons thinly sliced fresh basil

2 tablespoons chopped fresh tarragon leaves

3 cloves thinly sliced garlic

2 teaspoons apple cider vinegar, or more to taste

1 tablespoon extra-virgin olive oil

6 button mushrooms, fluted if desired

For the spicy bread crumbs:

1 tablespoon extra-virgin olive oil

1 small clove garlic, minced

3 tablespoons panko bread crumbs

Pinch of dried chile flakes

Pinch of celery seeds

2 teaspoons minced parsley leaves

Salt

For the herb salad and to finish:

1 tablespoon chopped celery leaves

1 tablespoon chopped parsley

1 tablespoon chopped chives

Squeeze of fresh lemon juice

Drizzle of extra-virgin olive oil

To make the mushroom roll: Preheat oven to 400°F. Line a baking sheet with parchment paper. Arrange portobello caps on baking sheet so that they slightly overlap. Using a pastry brush, generously brush the mushrooms with melted duck fat. Sprinkle mushrooms with the thyme leaves and salt and pepper. Cover the mushrooms with another piece of parchment, set another baking sheet on top to weight mushrooms down, and roast for 15 minutes. Remove from oven and set aside to cool.

In a medium bowl, combine crab, mayonnaise, and gruyère. Add more mayonnaise if needed to bind the crab and cheese. Season with salt and pepper. Remove 2 tablespoons of the filling and set aside for serving.

Lay a 12-inch piece of plastic wrap on a clean working surface. About 2 inches from the bottom left-hand corner of the plastic wrap, lay one mushroom slice vertically so the slice is tallest from top to bottom. Add another slice to the right of the first slice, overlapping a bit. Continue overlapping until you have an 8-inch row, from left to right, of mushroom slices.

Spoon crab filling in a line down the center of the line of mushroom slices. Using the plastic wrap, roll the mushrooms into a cigar-like shape, tying off the plastic wrap at the ends like a piece of candy. Secure ends with kitchen twine.

To make the tomato marinade: Combine all ingredients except the mushrooms in a medium bowl. Let sit at room temperature for an hour.

Strain the tomato liquid into a small saucepan. Taste and adjust salt, sugar, and/or vinegar to achieve a tangy marinade. Add mushrooms to the pan and set over medium heat. Bring to

a simmer, then remove pan from heat and let mushrooms cool in liquid.

For the spicy bread crumbs: In a small skillet, heat olive oil over medium heat. Add the garlic and sauté until just turning golden, about 3 minutes. Add the bread crumbs, chile flakes, celery seeds, and parsley. Gently toss to coat in oil and, stirring constantly, toast the bread crumbs until golden. Season with salt.

For the herb salad and to finish the dish: Fill a large saucepan with water. Set over high heat and bring to a boil. Turn heat to medium-high and add the wrapped mushroom roll to the water.

Cook the mushroom roll for 15 minutes and remove from water with tongs.

In a small bowl, toss together herbs with lemon juice and olive oil.

Carefully unwrap the mushroom roll and set it in the center of a large, shallow bowl. Spoon the reserved crab filling in six dots around the bowl and nestle a marinated mushroom into each dot. Stir the tomato marinade and spoon a bit of it into the bowl. Sprinkle the mushroom roll generously with the spicy bread crumbs. Divide the herb salad around the bowl. Serve immediately.

German Potato Salad

(SERVES 6)

For the dill pickle vinaigrette:

½ cup diced dill pickles

2 small shallots, minced

½ cup dill pickle juice

¼ cup distilled white vinegar

Juice of 2 lemons

¼ cup pickled mustard seeds (optional; see Pickled
   Mustard Seeds recipe on p. 43)

1 teaspoon chile flakes

1 cup canola oil

½ cup extra-virgin olive oil

*For the roast-carrot buttermilk puree and glazed
   carrots:*

6 medium peeled carrots, divided

3 tablespoons melted unsalted butter, divided

Salt

2 tablespoons buttermilk, or more if necessary

1 tablespoon water

½ teaspoon sugar

For the potato and cauliflower:

Salt

6 whole baby new potatoes

6 florets cheddar (orange) or white cauliflower

To assemble the salad:

½ cup sauerkraut

1 soft-boiled egg

1 tablespoon unsalted butter

1 smoked bratwurst, cooked

Dill fronds, for garnish

To make the dill pickle vinaigrette: In a medium
bowl, whisk together all ingredients.

For the roast-carrot buttermilk puree: Preheat
oven to 400°F. Line a baking sheet with
parchment paper. Lay 4 carrots on a baking
sheet and drizzle with 2 tablespoons of the
melted butter. Roll around to coat, sprinkle with
salt, and roast for 15–20 minutes or until tender
and browned in spots.

Puree carrots and buttermilk in a blender until
very smooth and velvety, adding a bit more
buttermilk if needed. Reserve.

For the glazed carrots: Cut the remaining 2
carrots into ½-inch slices. In a 10-inch skillet,
combine the carrots, remaining tablespoon of
melted butter, water, pinch of salt, and sugar
and set over medium heat. When water boils, stir
the carrots around as water reduces and butter
forms a glaze on the carrots, 7–10 minutes. The
carrots should be tender and the butter should
not break. Set aside to cool.

For the potatoes and cauliflower: Fill a large
saucepan with water; add salt until water tastes
like the sea. Set over high heat and bring to a boil.
Cook potatoes in the water until just tender (time
will vary depending on the size of the potatoes).
With a slotted spoon, remove potatoes from
water to a baking sheet and cool.

Add cauliflower to the same pot of boiling water
and cook until tender crisp, about 5 minutes
(again, time will vary depending on size of florets).
Transfer cauliflower to the same plate and cool.

To assemble: Preheat oven to 170°F. Set out a
large serving plate. Spread the carrot-buttermilk
puree onto the plate artfully; swoosh if you must.
Gently heat the glazed carrots, potatoes, and
cauliflower in the oven to take the chill off of

them. When warm, toss them in the dill pickle vinaigrette and arrange on the puree. Sprinkle the plate with some of the sauerkraut.

Set egg in a cup of hot tap water to warm it a bit. Meanwhile, in a small skillet over medium heat, melt butter and, when butter is hot, add

bratwurst and fry until nicely browned and slightly crispy.

Add brat to the plate. Carefully peel egg and add to the plate. Garnish salad with dill fronds and serve.

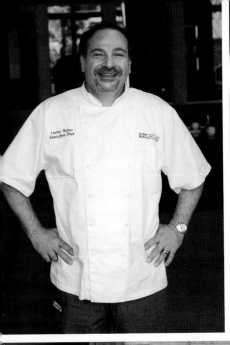

MARKET HOURS
TUESDAY - SUNDAY
9 AM - 9 PM
CLOSED MONDAY
& HOLIDAYS

Heartland Restaurant & Farm Direct Market

289 E. 5th Street
St. Paul, MN 55101
(651) 669-3536
HEARTLANDRESTAURANT.COM
Owner/Executive Chef: Lenny Russo

My first meal at Heartland Restaurant was in 2007, during a taping of an episode of Travel Channel's *Bizarre Foods*. Host Andrew Zimmern lives in the Twin Cities and was showcasing Minnesota, including the nationally recognized butchery and cooking mastery of Heartland's Executive Chef Lenny Russo. I was thrilled to be part of the show, especially after we sat down to an incredible nose-to-tail wild boar feast, including luscious, creamy brains and crispy fried testicles. Most memorably for me, Russo shared the boar's story, from the moment it arrived at Heartland through the butchery and preparation of each dish.

Among a long (long!) list of accomplishments, Russo is a three-time semifinalist for the James Beard Award for Best Chef Midwest. He recently completed a food diplomacy mission on behalf of the US Embassy in Ljubljana, Slovenia; was named to the US State Department's American Chef Corps; was included in the ranking of Best Chefs in America; and is a member of the St. Paul Area Chamber of Commerce Board of Directors. All of the accolades honor the fact that Russo has been cooking in the Twin Cities for more than thirty years, honing his contemporary take on Midwest cuisine at several beloved Twin Cities restaurants before opening Heartland in 2002.

Since my first Russo meal, Heartland has moved to Lowertown St. Paul near the St. Paul Farmers' Market and expanded both its footprint and name to Heartland Restaurant and Farm Market Direct. Occupying a whopping eighteen thousand square feet of a warehouse built at the turn of the last century, Heartland 2.0—with its soaring atrium, hand-crafted fixtures, etched glass, and Mission-style seating—is easily one of the most beautiful restaurants and catering spaces in the Twin Cities. While Heartland Restaurant's seasonally driven, constantly changing menu format remains the same, Heartland Farm Market Direct offers shoppers access to the same locally sourced, farm-fresh ingredients supplying the restaurant, as well as Heartland-branded prepared soups, stocks, charcuterie, and other deli treats for assembling artisanal meals at home.

Because running Heartland while championing local food and family farms isn't enough to keep him busy, Russo has also penned a column for the *Star Tribune* and recently announced that he's writing a cookbook titled *Heartland: Farm-Forward Dishes from the Great Midwest*, to be published in 2014.

GRILLED LAKE TROUT WITH BRAISED TURNIP GREENS & YOGURT SAUCE

(SERVES 6)

For the yogurt sauce:

12 ounces plain lowfat or whole-milk yogurt
½ cup coarsely chopped green onions
2 tablespoons chopped fresh dill
2 tablespoons olive oil
1 tablespoon freshly squeezed lemon juice
1 teaspoon sea salt
½ teaspoon freshly ground black pepper

For the trout:

6 (4- to 6-ounce) lake trout fillets
2 tablespoons vegetable oil
Sea salt and freshly ground black pepper
1 tablespoon unsalted butter
2 garlic cloves, minced
6 cups turnip greens, stemmed
½ teaspoon ground nutmeg
1 cup court bouillon

To make the yogurt sauce: In a medium glass bowl, stir together the yogurt, green onions, dill, olive oil, lemon juice, sea salt, and black pepper. Set aside.

To make the trout: Preheat grill.

Rub fillets on both sides with vegetable oil and season with salt and pepper. Grill trout over medium-high heat until medium-rare, about 5 minutes per side (adjust according to your grill). Transfer trout to a cutting board or large platter and let rest while you prepare the turnip greens.

In a 12-inch skillet over medium-low heat, melt the butter. Add garlic and sweat until tender, about 3 minutes. Add turnip greens, season with ½ teaspoon salt, ¼ teaspoon pepper, and nutmeg. Stir in the court bouillon. Bring to a simmer, cover pan, and braise greens until just tender, about 2 minutes. Remove from heat.

To serve: Divide greens evenly among six dinner plates. Nestle trout atop the greens, then spoon sauce over the trout.

Highland Grill

771 Cleveland Avenue South
St. Paul, MN 55116
(651) 690-1173
HIGHLANDGRILL.COM
CO-OWNERS: Stephanie Shimp and David Burley
Chef: Martha Sipma

Highland Grill co-owners Stephanie Shimp and David Burley met when they were both working as servers at The Nicollet Island Inn. After shifts they would put up their feet and dream of someday opening their own place. Not only did they make that dream happen, but they've gone on to open several successful restaurants around the Twin Cities under the banner of the Blue Plate Restaurant Company. Each spot genuinely reflects the neighborhood it's located in, with a variety of personalities and themes, but always with a focus on approachable, home-style fare fit for the whole family.

The restaurant that started it all is the Highland Grill in St. Paul's Highland Park neighborhood. The doors opened in 1993, and to this day you can find smiling neighbors cheerily waiting in line for a hearty, flavor-packed weekend brunch served with a smile. Signature dishes include a peanut- and jalapeño-studded turkey burger, tender potato-stuffed pierogi, crispy fried green beans, and killer fluffy pancakes.

Whether neighbors need a place to lunch with lady friends, a cozy post-movie nosh, a happy-hour cocktail with oysters on the half shell, or an everyone-is-happy breakfast with the kids, they often find themselves inside a Blue Plate restaurant, whether in Minneapolis or St. Paul.

BLUEBERRY OATMEAL PANCAKES

(MAKES ABOUT 12 PANCAKES)

1½ cups rolled oats

1 cup cake flour

1½ teaspoons baking powder

¾ teaspoon baking soda

½ teaspoon salt

1 tablespoon sugar

2 cups buttermilk

2 large eggs

4 tablespoons melted unsalted butter (½ stick), plus
   more for the skillet

1 cup fresh blueberries, rinsed and dried

Soft or melted unsalted butter and warm maple syrup,
   for serving

In a medium bowl, stir together rolled oats, cake flour, baking powder, baking soda, salt, and sugar. Set aside.

In a separate large bowl, whisk together buttermilk, eggs, and melted butter until smooth.

Add dry ingredients to the buttermilk-egg mixture, and with a spatula or big spoon, gently stir until just combined; do not overmix.

It's important to not skip this step: Let the batter rest for at least 5 minutes to thicken. You might feel like you should remix the batter after letting it sit, but don't—batter should be bubbly and thick.

While the batter rests, set a 12-inch skillet or griddle pan over medium-high heat. When batter is ready and skillet is hot, brush butter on the skillet and then ladle batter for one or two 4-inch pancakes into the pan. Scatter a few blueberries over the pancakes.

When pancakes are covered with little bubbles (around 5 minutes) and golden brown, flip and cook on the other side for 2–3 minutes or until golden brown. Transfer to a plate and keep warm. Continue cooking the rest of pancakes.

To serve, top pancakes with soft or melted butter and warm maple syrup.

THE KENWOOD

2115 W. 21st Street
Minneapolis, MN 55405
(612) 377-3695
THEKENWOODRESTAURANT.COM
Owner/Executive Chef: Don Saunders

The last time I dined at The Kenwood, our group ordered a new dish off the menu, something Executive Chef Saunders had come up with just the day before. Our server wondered if we could wait one moment, as the chef had run an errand and would want to plate the dish himself. Moments later, Saunders breezed into the dining room, grinned and waved a quick hello, then went into the kitchen and emerged with the new dish. This personal, warm atmosphere is based on experience, not luck. The Kenwood—opened since 2012 and named for the grand old Minneapolis neighborhood that surrounds it—is Saunders's third venture (Fugaise and In Season came before), and he and his staff have found their sweet spot.

The Kenwood is open all day, drawing local families for breakfast, business doers, and ladies who linger over bottles of bubbles (ahem) for lunch, and in the evening, when

dimmed lights glow softly against the plaid-cloth-covered walls, couples and groups of friends for dinner. On weekends, The Kenwood is jammed with young and old fans of perfect pancakes, topped with black walnut butter and drenched in local maple syrup. Dishes like roasted lamb loin with soisson beans, cardoons, and ramps, and a deep-fried duck egg with morel mushrooms and peas exemplify Saunders's cooking style—seasonal, fresh, and refined but never stuffy. The Kenwood is firmly a neighborhood restaurant; in fact, it's the neighborhood restaurant everyone wishes they had, a place to enjoy with your kids, take your mom for a special occasion, or savor a romantic dinner with your love. The staff remembers your name, you want to order every item on the menu, and the lovely setting can float from sunny casual to romantic without missing a beat. I confess I'm lucky enough to claim this gem as my neighborhood's own—my perfect Saturday includes a walk around Lake of the Isles and lunch at The Kenwood.

Butternut Panna Cotta with Fall Salad

(SERVES 8)

For the panna cotta:

3 large butternut squash, halved lengthwise and seeded
4 cups heavy cream
2 cups whole milk
½ teaspoon ground star anise
½ teaspoon ground cloves
½ teaspoon ground allspice
½ cup maple syrup
1 teaspoon salt
16 grams agar (can be found at Asian markets or online)

For the fall salad:

1 cup brussels sprouts leaves
1 cup chopped radicchio
¼ cup golden raisins
¼ cup pepitas, toasted
½ cup diced Honey Crisp apple
1 tablespoon apple cider vinegar
2 tablespoons pumpkinseed oil
Salt and freshly ground pepper

To make the panna cotta: Preheat oven to 350°F. Line two baking sheets with parchment paper and arrange squash, cut side down, on the sheets. Roast for 45–60 minutes, or until flesh is soft.

Using a spoon, scoop flesh from squash to measure 4 cups (reserve remaining squash for another use). In a dutch oven or other large pot, combine squash, cream, milk, spices, maple syrup, and salt and set over medium heat. Bring to a boil, then strain mixture through a fine-mesh strainer into a large bowl; discard strained solids.

Return mixture to the pot, stir in the agar, and bring back to a boil. Pour mixture into serving-size molds (ramekins, silicone molds, or even coffee cups).

Cover with plastic wrap and refrigerate panna cotta overnight.

To make the fall salad: In a medium bowl, toss together brussels sprouts leaves, radicchio, raisins, pepitas, and apple.

In a small bowl, whisk together the vinegar and pumpkinseed oil. Season to taste with salt and pepper. Pour dressing over salad and toss to coat.

To serve: Run a knife around the edges of the molds, invert over a plate, and give a firm side-to-side shake to loosen. Serve with fall salad.

LA BELLE VIE

510 GROVELAND AVENUE
MINNEAPOLIS, MN 55403
(612) 874-6440
LABELLEVIE.US
CO-OWNERS: TIM MCKEE AND WILLIAM SUMMERVILLE
EXECUTIVE CHEF: TIM MCKEE
CHEF DE CUISINE: MICHAEL DECAMP

When Executive Chef Tim McKee opened La Belle Vie in 1998, it wasn't his goal to set the standard for fine dining in the Twin Cities. But that's exactly what he's done, with a 2009 James Beard Award for Best Chef Midwest, a group of award-winning chefs working with him, and wide acceptance of La Belle Vie as the best restaurant in Minnesota. With a move in 2003 to the historic 510 Groveland building in downtown Minneapolis, La Belle Vie blossomed from a very delicious small-town gem into a big-city player, elegant and charming and utterly special, due in no small part to the service and wine program under the direction of Bill Summerville.

McKee has also built a reputation for training and launching some of the best chefs in the Twin Cities. Jack Riebel (Butcher & the Boar), Jamie Malone (Sea Change), and Erik Anderson (formerly of Sea Change and Catbird Seat in Nashville) have gone on to win their own recognition, but they all count time in McKee's kitchen as giving them a valuable start.

James Beard Award for Best Chef Midwest 2013 semifinalist Michael DeCamp (pictured) and Pastry Chef Diane Yang are putting their stamp on La Belle Vie these days, stacking up awards and delighting diners in both the chic formal dining room and sparkling romantic lounge. With dishes ranging from olive oil–poached halibut with saffron fumet and marrow-crusted asparagus to hands down the best potato chips anywhere, DeCamp has a grasp on the ethereal as well as homey (if fried chicken bathed in lavender honey is on the menu, order it without question). Yang's delightful, playful creations light up Instagram (follow her for a peek into pastry behind the scenes) as well as palates.

It would be a huge mistake to relegate La Belle Vie—as gorgeous and special as it is—to special-occasion dining only. The above-mentioned lounge is just right any night of the week—La Belle Vie is open every evening—which I can attest to because I have spent many, many happy hours sipping extraordinary cocktails and eating beautiful food with friends at the bar, in front of the fireplace, or at the Ottoman Empire (the nickname given to the large lounging ottoman at the back of the room). The cocktail program is one of the finest in town and includes both booze-full and booze-free options.

Rabbit Agnolotti

(SERVES 4–6)

For the rabbit filling:

8 rabbit legs
Salt
1 tablespoon olive oil
1 yellow onion, diced
2 carrots, diced
2 ribs celery, sliced
2 cups red wine
Water, as needed
2 cloves of garlic, smashed
1 tablespoon black peppercorns
Sprig of fresh thyme
¼ cup cooked lacinato kale, minced
½ cup caramelized onions, minced
¼ cup mascarpone cheese
2 tablespoons fresh thyme leaves
Freshly ground black pepper

For the pasta dough:

2 large eggs
2 large egg yolks
2 cups all-purpose flour, plus more for kneading

For filling the pasta:

1 large egg beaten with 1 tablespoon water
Pasta dough
Rabbit filling
Flour for dusting

For serving:

2 tablespoons soft unsalted butter

To make the rabbit filling: Preheat oven to 250°F. Season rabbit legs with a generous amount of salt. Heat a 12-inch, high-sided oven-safe skillet with a lid over medium-high heat. Add oil and, when oil is hot, add rabbit legs and brown on all sides. Remove legs to a large plate. Add the onion, carrots, and celery to the pan and sauté for 1 minute, stirring constantly. Add the wine and stir to deglaze the pan. Add the rabbit legs back to the pan and add water to cover. Add garlic cloves, black peppercorns, and thyme. Bring water to a simmer, then cover pan and place in oven. Braise legs until the rabbit is falling apart and tender, 2–3 hours. Cool.

Pick 2 cups of meat (discarding skin and bones) from the braised rabbit legs and chop by hand until meat starts to homogenize into a paste. Add the kale, caramelized onions, mascarpone, and thyme and season to taste with salt and pepper. Mix well and set aside.

To make the pasta dough: In a medium bowl, beat eggs and yolks with a fork until combined. Add the flour to the mixture and, using your hands, work until loosely combined. Turn out onto a lightly floured counter and knead for 10–15 minutes.

Wrap in plastic and let rest for 30 minutes.

To fill the pasta: Set out a baking sheet dusted with flour. Using a pasta roller, roll pasta dough into 12-inch sheets on the thinnest setting; lay sheets on flour-dusted counter as you go. Cut each sheet into 2-inch-wide strips. Working one strip at a time, brush strip with egg wash or water if you prefer. Place a tablespoon of filling about every ½ inch. Fold one side of the pasta over the filling, then fold the other side over to cover. With your fingers, press between the mounds of filling to remove all the air. Cut with fluted pasta cutter and pinch seams on the sides to make sure the agnolotti are sealed tightly. Transfer to baking sheet.

To cook the pasta and serve: Bring a large pot full of salted water to a boil over high heat. When the water boils, cook agnolotti for 3–4 minutes, until al dente, then drain in a colander.

Return agnolotti to pot and add butter. Toss gently to coat and serve immediately in warm bowls.

Lucia's Restaurant, Wine Bar, and To Go

1432 W. 31st Street
Minneapolis, MN 55408
(612) 825-1572
lucias.com
Owner/Executive Chef: Lucia Watson

It's hard to believe that Lucia's Restaurant has been a part of the Minneapolis culinary scene for nearly three decades. Although the restaurant has expanded to include a Wine Bar and Lucia's To Go, each dish remains as fresh and inspired as the day the restaurant opened and first captured the hearts of Minnesotans in search of best-quality food. It's fair to say that Executive Chef Watson is one of the founders—if not the founder—of the sustainable agriculture and farm-to-table movement in Minnesota. She has inspired, trained, and launched the careers of dozens of chefs in both Minneapolis and St. Paul, all while overseeing her own steady—and delicious—operation.

Watson spends part of her time in Brittany, France, returning to Minnesota with new flavors and ideas for her restaurants. Despite being repeatedly nominated for the James Beard Award for Best Chef Midwest, Watson remains one of the most charming and gracious hosts in the Twin Cities, qualities imbued into the very walls of

her establishments. Lucia's softly peach-hued dining room glows with warm sunshine, always adorned with spectacular fresh flowers. It is my favorite ladies' lunch spot in town; the light is flattering, the seasonally driven menu (which changes weekly) is elegant and nourishing, the wine pairings are some of the best in town, the service is top-notch, and the room is always pleasantly abuzz.

Watson carries her passion for a sustainable food system beyond her restaurants. She served a four-year term on the Organic Advisory Task Force to the Minnesota Department of Agriculture and is a former board member of the Chef's Collaborative. In addition, she has served as board chair for the Youth Farm and Market Project as well as the Institute for Agriculture and Trade Policy. Watson teaches and speaks throughout the year, often in support of sustainability and farming issues. In addition, she has coauthored two popular cookbooks: *Savoring the Seasons of the Northern Heartland*, with Beth Dooley, and most recently, *Cooking Freshwater Fish*.

But in the end, her passion begins and ends with hospitality. From a love for food that began with cooking with her grandmother, her passion remains "the true sense of hospitality, welcoming the guests, nurturing them with good healthy food and ambience, making them comfortable and happy." Here's to doing exactly that for another thirty years!

WILD RICE PANCAKES WITH CRANBERRY SALSA

(SERVES 4–6)

For the cranberry salsa:

1 cup fresh or frozen cranberries
1 tablespoon grated fresh ginger
2 cloves garlic
1 jalapeño pepper, seeded
Juice and zest of ½ lime, or to taste
4–5 tablespoons sugar, or to taste
¼ cup chopped fresh cilantro
2 scallions, chopped

For the wild rice pancakes:

2 cups cooked wild rice
¼ cup all-purpose flour
1 large egg
1 scallion, finely chopped
⅓ cup milk
Salt and freshly ground pepper
½ teaspoon minced fresh thyme leaves
Vegetable oil, for skillet

To make the salsa: Combine all ingredients in the bowl of a food processor. Pulse until mixture is a roughly chopped puree. Adjust seasoning, adding more sugar or lime to taste, if desired. Can be made 1 day ahead; cover and refrigerate.

To make the wild rice pancakes: Stir together all of the ingredients (except vegetable oil) in a large mixing bowl until just combined.

Heat a large skillet or pancake griddle over medium-high heat. When pan is hot, brush with a bit of oil. Cook one small pancake and taste—adjust the liquid or flour to taste; batter consistency can vary depending on the texture of the cooked wild rice. Pancakes should be crispy, golden, and cooked all the way through. Serve hot with cranberry salsa.

The Lynn on Bryant

5003 Bryant Avenue South
Minneapolis, MN 55419
(612) 767-7797
THELYNNONBRYANT.COM
Owner/Executive Chef: Peter Ireland

Despite our epic winters, Minneapolis–St. Paul is a pretty terrific place to live and eat, and as such, every once in a while we steal a terrific chef from another city. Not that there aren't plenty of home-grown stars, it's just good to inject new ideas and a fresh perspective into any city's dining scene. The Twin Cities lucked out when Executive Chef Peter Ireland's wife, Rebecca, decided upon law school here in Minnesota. A Vermont native with years of cooking experience in top kitchens from France to Beijing to New York, Ireland landed at Minneapolis luxury foods purveyor Great Ciao for two years while pulling together the idea for The Lynn.

Ireland's then-partner Jay Peterson launched a successful Kickstarter campaign in 2012 to raise funds toward opening The Lynn, with the goal of "reestablishing connections to small farms and sustainable living, and of bringing family, friends, and neighbors together for a delicious meal."

The Lynnhurst neighborhood of Minneapolis was thrilled when those plans for the space were revealed. The building that houses The Lynn sadly burned to the ground in 2010, displacing not one but two well-loved, highly regarded restaurants. When both owners announced relocation plans for different parts of the city, residents wondered if they'd lost not one but two spots for top-notch dining near home.

They needn't have worried. The Lynn hit the ground running with elegant-yet-comfy brunch, lunch, and dinner menus. Egg lovers delight in the farm-fresh omelet, eggs in a jar, or croque madame topped with a fried egg. Date-night diners swoon for the house pâtée, grass-fed burger on a homemade English muffin with perfect fries, or duck confit with warm lentil salad. Vegetarians and gluten-free diners are grateful for many flavorful choices, including addictive chickpea fries, bountiful salads, and decadent house-made pastries.

The Lynnhurst neighborhood is a family-friendly haven near the Minneapolis chain of lakes, miles of walking and bike trails, several

coffee (8 oz/12 oz)

KOPPLINS HOUSE BLEND	2.25/3.25
CAFE AU LAIT	2.25/3.25
ESPRESSO	2.25
AMERICANO	2.50/3.50
MACCHIATO	2.50
CAPPUCINO	3.25
LATTE	3.50/4.00
MOCHA	4.00/5.00
MIEL	3.75/4.50
ICED AMERICANO	3.00
ICED LATTE (12 oz.)	4.00
ICED MOCHA (12 oz.)	5.00

beverages

HOT TEA	2.25
ICED TEA	2.50
HOUSEMADE CHAI	3.25/4.00
ICED CHAI	4.00
HOT COCOA	4.00/5.00
HOUSEMADE SODAS	2.25
MEXICAN COKE	2.00
DIET COKE	3.00
ORANGE JUICE	3.00
WHOLE MILK	2.50
CHOCOLATE MILK	3.00
SPARKLING H2O	0.95 (carafe: 2.95)

Ask for Beer & Wine List

Specials du Jour

Soup: WHITE BEAN & BACON   CAULIFLOWER Omelet   APPLE Baked Pancake   Eggs BENEDICT

beautiful parks, the Lake Harriet band shell, and picturesque Minnehaha Creek. Given the setting, and Ireland's love of the outdoors, it made complete sense for The Lynn to offer not just an extensive menu of takeaway dishes for busy families but also picnic baskets for a day spent doing what Minnesotans do best: spending every minute of every not-cold day in the sun.

MAPLE VINEGAR–GLAZED CHICKEN LEGS WITH VEGETABLES

(SERVES 6)

For the chicken:

6 chicken legs with thighs attached (call butcher ahead to request)
Salt and freshly ground pepper
2 tablespoons vegetable oil
1½ cups apple cider vinegar
1½ cups maple syrup
2 tablespoons unsalted butter

For the celery root puree:

6 cups water
Salt
1 cup milk
3 cups diced peeled celery root
1 cup diced peeled russet potato
¼ cup olive oil
½ cup heavy cream, warmed
Freshly ground pepper

For the carrots and radishes:

5 tablespoons unsalted butter, divided
2 cloves garlic, peeled, divided
2 sprigs fresh thyme, divided
2 sprigs fresh rosemary, divided
2 cups (1-inch slices) peeled carrots
Salt and pepper
2 cups trimmed and halved radishes

To prepare the chicken: Preheat oven to 350°F. Pat the chicken legs dry with paper towels and season generously with salt and pepper.

Set a large cast-iron skillet over medium-high heat. Add the oil and, when the oil is hot and shimmering, add the chicken legs, skin side down. Sear until skin is golden brown, about 5 minutes, then turn the legs. Add the vinegar and syrup to the pan and transfer to the oven.

Bake chicken for 45 minutes or until chicken is very tender. Remove chicken legs to a warm platter, transferring skillet with pan juices to a burner over medium-high heat. Reduce juices until thick and syrupy and bubbles are slow to break, then swirl in the butter to finish.

While the chicken cooks, make the celery root puree and glazed vegetables.

To make the celery root puree: Set out two large saucepans. Add 3 cups of water to each pan and salt to taste. Add milk to one of the pans. Add celery root to the pan with milk; add potato to the other pan. Place both pans over medium-high heat and bring to a boil. Turn heat to low and simmer until celery root and potatoes are tender when pierced with a knife; times will vary between the two.

Drain and pass each through a ricer, returning both riced celery root and potato together to one of the two saucepans. Stir in olive oil and cream, season with salt and pepper, and keep warm.

To make the glazed carrots: Set a 10-inch skillet over medium-high heat. Add 2 tablespoons butter to the pan and, when butter is melted, add 1 clove garlic and 1 sprig each of thyme and rosemary. Heat until fragrant, about 2 minutes, then stir in carrots and a bit of salt.

Sauté the carrots with the herbs and garlic, stirring continually, until carrots are tender. Season with salt and pepper and transfer to a bowl.

To make the glazed radishes: Set the same 10-inch skillet over medium-high heat. Add 2 tablespoons butter to the pan and, when butter is hot, add the remaining garlic clove and remaining sprigs of thyme and rosemary. Add the radishes and repeat the process above, tossing the radishes continually until tender. Season with salt and pepper and add radishes to the bowl of carrots.

To serve: Divide celery root puree among six warm shallow bowls. Top with chicken legs and spoon pan sauce over chicken. Divide glazed vegetables among bowls (discarding herb sprigs and garlic cloves), alongside the chicken.

I couldn't write a book about good food without including a few of the farms that feed us most beautifully. The overall trend is downward for small family farms, but there are exceptions to this rule, farms who've crafted careful relationships with chefs and restaurants and families to grow sustainable and organic meat, vegetables, and dairy products while providing for their families, too. There are several Twin Cities–area farms doing it with style and grace, providing some of the best ingredients in the world for us to eat. I would spend my whole life photographing farms if I could; I'm not sure why it calls so strongly to me. My grandparents grew up on farms, but they were townsfolk by the time I knew them. Maybe it's because I appreciate so much about good food and carefully grown ingredients—and because it's important to my health to know where my food comes from.

Whatever the reason, it is a joy to spend the day at a place like Star Thrower Farm, where Deborah and Scott Pikovsky raise Icelandic sheep and make cheese, lamb, and wool products west of the Twin Cities. It's easy to see that Deborah has a very special connection with her animals, both the sheep and their guard llamas. Kerwyn the llama, in

particular, threatens to steal the show with his stern brown coat, unfathomably long eyelashes, and hilariously bossy personality. As lovely as it is to see Star Thrower's rolling pastures, fluffy sheep, and unforgettable barn, it's easier to chat with Deborah at Fulton or Mill City Farmers' Markets on summer weekends where she sells all four Star Thrower Farm cheeses as well as lamb and knitted wool products. See starthrowerfarm.com for dates and times.

I first visited Little Foot Farm while taking photographs ahead of an Outstanding in the Field farm dinner in 2012 and was instantly smitten. Karen Weiss and Sally Doherty's heritage-breed hog farm, east of the Twin Cities, is about as picture-perfect as farms come, with a cheerful red farmhouse as well as two darling young sons—and piglets!—underfoot. Karen works closely with Executive Chef Michael Phillips of Red Table Meat Company to provide best-quality, sustainably raised pork for his charcuterie. Little Foot Farm also sells pork, eggs, and vegetables to the public; see little-footfarm.com for ordering details.

The ladies of Bossy Acres know a thing or two about marketing, and I mean that in the best possible way. The convergence of farms and social media is a relatively new occurrence, and they work it wisely. With an active—and highly entertaining—Facebook and Twitter presence, Bossy K (Karla Pankow) and Bossy E (Elizabeth Millard) share their farming story and promote the merits of organic farming. Their popular CSA (community supported agriculture) shares sell out quickly each year, but you can find them at Kingfield and Mill City Farmers' Markets throughout the growing season. See bossyacres.com for dates, to volunteer, or to purchase Bossy gear.

Every city has its botanical treasures, and one of the Twin Cities' is the University of Minnesota's Landscape Arboretum. With more than 1,100 acres of breathtaking gardens and tree collections, as well as prairie, woods, miles of walking and hiking trails, and a special-event center, Minnesotans who love to garden or to stroll through flowers and trees flock to the Arboretum for inspiration, classes, and, in the autumn, apples. Starting in September, the Arboretum's AppleHouse sells a changing inventory of fifty varieties of apples—some, like the Honey Crisp, developed by the University of Minnesota—as

well as other specialty goods. There is no better way to spend a golden autumn afternoon than snapping pictures of the changing leaves and then heading home with a bag of apples to bake a pie. Check for apple varieties and hours at arboretum.umn.edu.

I fell in love with Riverbend Farm when they hosted not one but two farm dinners in one week in the summer of 2012. Greg and Mary Reynolds have been organic farming their fairytale-beautiful property on the North Fork of the Crow River west of Minneapolis since 1994, selling CSA produce shares as well as selling directly to co-ops and restaurants like Birchwood Cafe. In fact, Birchwood has a close relationship with Riverbend, gathering groups of volunteers for occasional "crop mobs" to help with weeding and harvesting. Children play games, grown-ups play farmer, and everyone enjoys a picnic at the end of the day. The Reynoldses are too humble to admit it, but they have many admirers in the farming and restaurant communities because of their land stewardship and mentoring practices. See rbfcsa.com for more information. And for a taste of farm-fresh food at home, try your hand at one of the recipes below.

Minnesota Landscape Arboretum, University of Minnesota

Scott Pampuch, District Executive Chef, University of Minnesota

Chicken Ballotine with Wild Mushroom & Date Stuffing

(SERVES 4)

For the chicken, wild mushroom, and date stuffing:

1¼ cups chicken stock

¼ teaspoon salt

½ ounce (about ½ cup) dried mushrooms, such as morel or lobster, rinsed and broken into pieces

1 cup (about ½ large) sliced leek

1 tablespoon olive oil

¼ cup water

1 pound ground chicken

4–5 whole, pitted dates, roughly chopped

To prepare the chicken:

1 (3¾-pound) chicken, skin-on, boned (call your butcher ahead if you don't want to do it yourself)

¼ teaspoon salt

¼ teaspoon freshly ground black pepper

Chicken, wild mushroom, and date stuffing (see recipe)

½ cup sparkling wine

½ cup chicken stock

1 celery stalk, cut into ¼-inch dice

½ cup chopped onion

1 carrot, peeled, cut into ¼-inch dice

1 tablespoon each chopped fresh flat-leaf parsley, tarragon, and chives

To make the chicken, wild mushroom, and date stuffing: Combine stock, salt, and dried mushrooms in a large saucepan and bring to a boil, then cover, reduce heat to low, and simmer for 10 minutes. Remove the mushrooms, reserving the liquid. Let mushrooms cool to room temperature.

Meanwhile, combine leek, oil, and water in a small saucepan and bring to a boil, then cover, reduce heat to low, and simmer for 8–10 minutes or until liquid has been reduced to a glaze. Cool to room temperature.

Place ground chicken in a large mixing bowl. Add cooled mushrooms, leeks, and dates and mix until incorporated evenly.

To prepare chicken: Lay the chicken skin side down on a clean work surface and season with salt and pepper. Spread the chicken, wild mushroom, and date stuffing evenly over the chicken. Roll the chicken up jelly-roll style, wrap tightly in plastic wrap, and refrigerate for 1 hour (or overnight) to firm up.

TWIN CITIES FARMS

Preheat oven to 400°F. Remove roll from refrigerator, remove plastic wrap, and truss the chicken ballotine with kitchen twine. Place ballotine on a rack in a roasting pan and roast for 1 hour, or until a thermometer inserted into the center of the roll reads 165°F. Transfer to a cutting board.

For the sauce: Skim away most of the fat from the drippings in the pan. Set the pan over medium heat, add the wine and chicken stock to the drippings, and bring to a simmer while stirring up the browned bits and juices to deglaze the pan.

Strain the juices into a small saucepan. Add the celery, onion, and carrot and bring to a boil over high heat. Cover, reduce heat to low, and simmer gently for 5 minutes. Strain the sauce once again, discarding vegetables and returning sauce to a boil. Turn heat to low and simmer until sauce thickens and coats the back of the spoon.

Cut string from ballotine. Slice into 1-inch thick slices. Stir chopped herbs into sauce and serve with ballotine.

MINNESOTA SQUASH, BEET & APPLE SALAD

(SERVES 4)

½ small butternut squash, peeled, seeded, and cut into
  ½-inch cubes
4 tablespoons extra-virgin olive oil, divided
2 medium Chioggia beets
1 medium red beet
1 medium golden beet
4 garlic cloves, peeled and smashed
2 sprigs fresh rosemary, halved

2 Meyer lemons, zested and juiced, reserved
  separately, divided
1 medium Honey Crisp apple
1 medium Braeburn apple
1 cup (3–4 ounces) sunflower sprouts
1 tablespoon apple cider vinegar
Coarse sea salt and freshly ground pepper

Preheat oven to 400°F. Line a baking sheet with parchment paper. In a large bowl, toss squash with 2 tablespoons olive oil. Spread squash on baking sheet and roast for 15 minutes. Turn squash pieces over and continue roasting until tender and browned in spots, about 10 minutes. Set aside to cool.

Trim beets and wrap each beet in foil with a clove of garlic and ½ rosemary sprig. Arrange wrapped beets on a baking and sheet and roast for 45 minutes, or until a knife pierces the beets with little resistance.

Remove beets from oven, let stand in the foil until cool enough to handle, then rub the beets with the foil until skin comes off. Discard skin,

garlic, and rosemary. Cut beets into ½-inch cubes and place in a large bowl. Add squash to the bowl, then add half the lemon juice and zest and toss to coat.

Cut apples into ½-inch cubes and place in a medium bowl. Add the remaining lemon juice and zest and toss to coat. Add sunflower sprouts and toss again.

In a small bowl, whisk together apple cider vinegar and remaining olive oil. Arrange beets and squash on a platter. Top with apples and sunflower sprouts. Drizzle with apple cider vinaigrette. Season with salt and pepper.

Star Thrower Farm

Deborah and Scott Pikovsky, Owners, Star Thrower Farm

Granola

(MAKES ABOUT 20 CUPS)

Note: The real secret to good granola (like many things) is to use really good ingredients. They use half the sugar that most recipes call for so the granola is not overly sweet and can be enjoyed with a dab of really good honey. It is terrific served with Star Thrower Farm skyr (a yogurt-like cheese).

250 grams (9 ounces) French unsalted butter with fleur de sel
115 grams (½ cup) honey
1 tablespoon Tahitian vanilla
2 pinches of Vietnamese or Ceylon cinnamon
2 pounds thick-cut gluten-free oats
2 cups shelled Arya pistachios
2 cups fried and salted Marcona almonds
2 cups whole pecans (from New Mexico if possible)
1½ cups brown sugar
2 cups dried cherries (from Door County, Wisconsin, if possible)
1 cup dried, unsweetened coconut flakes
French fleur de sel salt, to taste

Preheat oven to 280°F. In a 14-inch skillet over medium heat, melt butter with honey. Add vanilla and cinnamon, then add oats and gently brown. Add all nuts and brown sugar and mix well.

Transfer mixture to a baking sheet, spreading evenly. Bake for 20 minutes. Add cherries and coconut and bake for 10 more minutes, until granola is golden brown. Salt to taste and cool. Store in airtight container.

Manny's Tortas

920 E. Lake Street
Suite 125
Minneapolis, MN 55407
(612) 870-3930
mannystortas.com
Owner/Executive Chef: Manny Gonzalez

Ever since the Earl of Sandwich interrupted his card game, man has been working to make the stuff between two slices of bread better. Chef Manny Gonzalez's award-winning contribution to this effort—known as *tortas*—has earned a dedicated following in part because of proper construction and in part because of the man who makes them. Gonzalez, who owns the business along with his sister Victoria, is one of those rare people who makes the world a better place. His humor, smile, and kindness are

widely known and utterly infectious—it is not an exaggeration to say that it is a joy to visit with him. That makes it delicious bonus points that Manny's tortas—traditional Mexican sandwiches made of crusty bread layered with warm-and-cold fixings like tender meat, creamy beans, crunchy greens, kicky sauces, spicy pickles, and plenty of melting cheese— are as delightful as a day off.

After attending culinary school in Mexico, Gonzalez moved to Minneapolis to learn English with the intent to go back to Mexico and work in the hotel and tourism industry. But he started cooking while he was here, and making friends, and eventually he decided that despite the cold winters, he could envision a life in the Twin Cities. Gonzalez was presented with the opportunity to open his own restaurant in 1999, and he jumped at it, opening the first Manny's Tortas in Mercado Central in Minneapolis. He added a second operation in Midtown Global Market in 2006. And after ten years of applying, Gonzalez was accepted as a vendor at the Minnesota State Fair in 2010, where he's attracted a whole new crowd of enthusiastic fans, some of whom show up for Manny's annual Cinco de Manny cooking class at Kitchen in the Market.

Gonzalez says, "Food is one of the greatest pleasures in life." Everyone else thinks one of the greatest pleasures is Manny and his tortas.

MANNY'S SPECIAL TORTA

(MAKES 1 SANDWICH)

1 tablespoon soft unsalted butter

1 (6-inch) loaf French bread (or half a baguette), halved lengthwise

½ cup refried beans

1 tablespoon olive oil

¼ yellow onion, diced

½ ripe tomato, chopped

½ cup sliced button mushrooms

1 jalapeño pepper, trimmed and diced

Salt

3 thin slices ham

4 ounces steak, sliced thin

3 slices swiss cheese

½ ripe avocado

1 tablespoon chipotle mayonnaise (mayonnaise with adobo sauce, to taste, stirred in)

Place a 10-inch skillet over medium heat. When pan is hot, spread butter on cut sides of baguette and toast with cut sides down in pan until golden.

Transfer baguette halves to a serving plate, toasted side up, and return pan to heat. Add beans to the skillet and when they are hot, divide them between the two sides of baguette.

Return pan to the heat and add olive oil. When the oil is hot, add onions, tomatoes, mushrooms, and jalapeño. Sprinkle with a bit of salt. Sauté until softened, about 5 minutes, then distribute over half of the bread.

Return pan to the heat and add the ham and steak. Cook until steak is browning, then top with cheese slices and cook until cheese is melting. While cheese melts, add avocado slices to one side of the sandwich. Transfer ham, steak, and melted cheese to the other side of the sandwich. Squirt chipotle mayonnaise onto the cheese, press both sides of the sandwich together, and cut in half. Enjoy!

Meritage

410 St. Peter Street
St. Paul, MN 55102
(651) 222-5670
meritage-stpaul.com
Owner/Executive Chef: Russell Klein

Sitting in the dining room at Meritage, it's hard to believe that you aren't tucked inside a Paris brasserie. The tiled floor, cozy maroon seats, and gilded mirrors are so exquisitely, classically, casually French that when a server hands you an English menu, there's a brief moment of disappointment. But only brief! Executive Chef Russell Klein's menu reads like a list of all of my favorite foods: crispy frites, a stunning selection of oysters, cassoulet, and . . . an exquisite matzoh ball soup. Klein's wife, Desta, manages the front of house with easy, flawless service. Shortly after opening Meritage in 2007, the Kleins expanded to add a stunning bar, anchored by an antique absinthe dispenser, creating the best spot in either town for a romantic evening of oysters and craft cocktails.

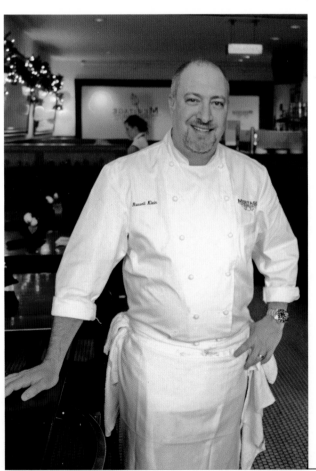

In the summer, Meritage guests flock to the patio for beautiful views of downtown St. Paul, stroll by the curbside crepe stand for a bite on the go, or spend a weekend day at one of the Twin Cities' premier outdoor food festivals: Oysterfest. It's a sight to behold to witness oyster shuckers and farms from both coasts of the United States descending upon St. Paul to feed legions of oyster-crazed Minnesotans. For pure fun alone, Meritage has earned its Best French Restaurant accolades from every publication in town, but it's the beauty and quality of the food that have earned Executive Chef Klein a James Beard Semifinalist nod. And lest Minneapolitans decide crossing the river to St. Paul is too far for their French fix, they can now settle into the Klein's latest venture: Brasserie Zentral in downtown Minneapolis opened in spring 2014.

Pimm's Provençal Cocktail

(MAKES 1 COCKTAIL)

1½ ounces lavender-infused gin (Sapphire preferred)
½ ounce Pimm's No. 1
½ ounce elderflower syrup
Splash of sour
2 dashes cherry bitters
Cherry, for garnish

Combine all ingredients but cherry in a shaker filled with ice. Shake and strain into a chilled martini glass. Garnish with cherry. Sip while you make French onion soup!

Soupe À l'Oignon Gratinée

CLASSIC FRENCH ONION SOUP

(SERVES 6)

½ cup (1 stick) unsalted butter

1½ pounds sweet yellow onions, thinly sliced (about 3–5 onions)

2 teaspoons minced garlic

1 cup dry red wine

1 gallon beef or chicken stock

Salt and freshly ground black peper

6 slices hearty sourdough or white bread

12 ounces gruyère cheese, grated

6–12 slices emmentaler cheese

Add butter to a large, heavy-bottomed pot and set over low heat. When butter is melted, add the onions and cook, stirring frequently, until onions are soft and have released their liquid.

Turn the heat to medium-low and continue cooking until the onions are golden brown. Do not rush the browning; take your time to slowly caramelize the onions, which brings out their natural sweetness. This step should take an hour or so.

Add the garlic and cook for another minute. Add the red wine and stir to loosen any browned bits on the bottom of the pan. Simmer until the red wine is almost evaporated. Add the stock and simmer for 30 minutes. Season to taste with salt and pepper.

While the soup simmers, arrange six oven-safe soup bowls or ramekins on a baking sheet. Trim the bread slices to fit the tops of the bowls. Lightly toast the bread. Preheat broiler.

Ladle the soup into the serving bowls, settle a piece of toasted bread on top, sprinkle with the grated cheese, and top with the sliced cheese.

Transfer baking sheet to oven and broil soup until cheese is melted, bubbling, and browned in spots. Serve immediately.

PICCOLO RESTAURANT

4300 BRYANT AVENUE SOUTH
MINNEAPOLIS, MN 55409
(612) 827-8111
PICCOLOMPLS.COM
OWNER/EXECUTIVE CHEF: DOUG FLICKER

There are those of us who overcomplicate things. A simple phone call turns into five e-mails, a text, and two private messages. Getting dressed for work results in several outfit changes, torn stockings, and a missing glove. Even attempts to declutter turn into boxes of things to give away that linger for weeks by the back door. And then there's Doug Flicker, who seems to have a preternatural ability to pare down and simplify. Dishes that in other kitchens might represent excess emerge sparkling and pure from Piccolo's. No one in the Twin Cities plates food more beautifully and with more restraint, a talent that inspires many other Minneapolis–St. Paul chefs.

It works synergistically, then, that Piccolo's name refers not just to the small size of the restaurant, but also to the small-plate style of the menu. It is not unreasonable for a group of four to order every item on the menu. With that many plates headed your way, it could be an overwhelming experience if each dish weren't so artfully composed and delightfully balanced in flavor and texture. But they are! Each plate is like a little gift, a food photographer's dream to photograph . . . and then devour.

I was a faithful fan of Flicker's first restaurant, Auriga, which closed in 2007 after a delicious ten-year run. Flicker opened Piccolo in 2010 to immediate acclaim, and the accolades have continued to stack up, including another semifinalist nod in 2014 for the James Beard Foundation Award for Best Chef Midwest.

But clearly Flicker is not cooking for the accolades. "What I enjoy most is working with the people that both work and dine at Piccolo—being a part of each others' lives and being there when they succeed and grow as cooks, servers, and people. Piccolo is on its third staff marriage, its second college graduation, and its third baby in less than four years. So much has happened in a short period of time."

Including opening a new spot last summer with his wife, Amy Greeley. Sandcastle is a top-notch summertime concession stand (their tag line is Eat Like a King) on the shores of Lake Nokomis in south Minneapolis. You could spend a pretty marvelous Saturday biking around the lake and stopping by Sandcastle for a lunch of Castle Rock organic cheese curds, the Dog Flicker (a Vienna-beef dog topped with kimchee and a fried egg), and fry bread with bison and white cheddar, all washed down with a local brew. Then bike home to burn off your lunch, shower and spiff up, and head to Piccolo for dinner and wine with friends, because Piccolo is a true Twin Cities gem, not to be missed.

Braised Octopus with Tête de Porc, Charred White Asparagus, Jalapeños & Garlic

(SERVES 4)

Chef Flicker's note: We love to use unusual ingredients like octopus and pig's head and pair them in unexpected ways. Consider this a basic recipe and technique for the dish, then feel free to alter it in any way to make it your own. Start the recipe the day before you plan to serve it.

For the octopus:

½ cup salt

¼ cup sugar

½ cup tomato paste, divided

3 tablespoons pimenton

2 gallons water

4–5 pounds octopus

3 carrots

3 celery stalks

1 onion

2 bay leaves

¼ cup distilled white vinegar

For the garlic puree and garlic chips:

10 garlic cloves, unpeeled

Sugar

Salt

Vegetable oil

6 garlic cloves, peeled and sliced as thinly as possible

For the charred asparagus and jalapeño:

12 white asparagus spears, peeled and bottom third trimmed away

Extra-virgin olive oil

Salt

1 jalapeño pepper

For the tête de porc and serving:

4 slices tête de porc (can be found in most Mexican or traditional butcher shops)

Octopus slices (see recipe)
Charred asparagus spears (see recipe)
Garlic puree (see recipe)
Jalapeño slices (see recipe)
Garlic chips (see recipe)

To prepare the octopus: In a large bowl or stockpot, stir together salt, sugar, ¼ cup tomato paste, pimenton, and water until salt and sugar are dissolved. Add octopus, cover, and refrigerate for 24 hours.

Remove octopus from brine (discard brine) and place in dutch oven or other medium-size pot. Add carrots, celery, onion, remaining ¼ cup tomato paste, bay leaves, and vinegar. Add water to cover the octopus by 1 inch. Set pot over medium-high heat and bring to a boil, then reduce heat to low so liquid is gently simmering. Cook octopus for approximately 90 minutes or until tender.

Remove octopus from the cooking liquid (discard liquid), set on a large plate or baking sheet, and refrigerate until octopus is cold, 1–2 hours. Remove tentacles from the head (discard head). Slice tentacles into 2-inch pieces.

To make the garlic puree and garlic chips: While the octopus chills, add 10 unpeeled garlic cloves to a small saucepan, cover with water, and bring to a boil. Turn heat to low and simmer for 25 minutes. Remove cloves from cooking liquid (reserve liquid) and cool to room temperature.

Peel cloves and puree in a blender, adding cooking liquid if needed, to create a smooth, thick sauce. Season to taste with a bit of sugar and salt. Transfer to a squeeze bottle.

Set out a paper-towel-lined plate. In a small saucepan, heat vegetable oil to approximately 250°F. When oil is hot, add garlic slices and stir continuously to prevent garlic slices from sticking together. Adjust heat as needed for garlic to bubble and start to brown. As soon as the garlic slices start to change color, remove them from oil and drain on paper-towel-lined plate. Season with salt.

To make the charred asparagus and jalapeño: Set out a paper-towel-lined plate. Heat a 12-inch nonstick skillet over high heat, allowing pan to get very hot. Add asparagus to the pan without shaking or turning and cook until asparagus starts to burn or char. Add a couple drops of extra-virgin olive oil to the pan, which will create a bit of smoke and extra char. Remove asparagus

from pan and transfer to paper-towel-lined plate. Season with salt.

With a small paring knife, cut the stem end off the jalapeño. With the tip of the knife or a small demitasse spoon, remove seeds and membrane from inside the pepper. Cut pepper into 8 slices. Reserve in ice water until needed.

To make the tête de porc and serve: Arrange 1 slice of tête de porc on each of four plates.

Heat a 12-inch nonstick skillet over medium-high heat. Once pan is hot, add the octopus. Sear octopus on each side for 2–3 minutes, or until octopus starts to color; octopus is already cooked so this is just for heat and color. Divide warm octopus among the plates. Divide asparagus spears among the plates, propping them against the octopus to give height to the dish. Add dots of garlic puree around the plate. Prop jalapeño slices on the octopus and asparagus. Finish with a garnish of garlic chips.

PIZZERIA LOLA

5557 XERXES AVENUE SOUTH
MINNEAPOLIS, MN 55410
(612) 424-8338

PIZZERIALOLA.COM
OWNER/EXECUTIVE CHEF: ANN KIM
CO-OWNER: CONRAD LEIFUR

In just a few short years, Pizzeria Lola has achieved cult status in the Twin Cities for serving some of the best pizza in the country. And it's not just Minnesotans who think so: Lola was recently listed as one of *Food & Wine* magazine's Best Pizza Places in the United States. So why do people crowd the patio waiting for a table when there's a perfectly lovely restaurant next door? (Aside: The residents of Minneapolis's Fulton neighborhood are lucky indeed to have Pizzeria Lola plus next-door-neighbor Cave Vin within walking distance. The rest of the city is jealous.) It's the pizza, of course—wood-fire

blistered, with best-quality, innovative toppings that represent scratch cooking—as well as Executive Chef Ann Kim's Korean heritage.

But it's also this simple and too-often overlooked touch: It is fun to eat at Pizzeria Lola, for diners of all ages. Parents can order a glass of wine and send their children off to the photo booth for goofy-faced shenanigans. Teens can show up with prom dates (yes, my son and his friend took their prom dates to Lola) and are treated like kings and queens. Everyone can admire the stunning, copper beauty that is the pizza oven, the glamorous centerpiece of the restaurant, twinkling with the lights reflected off the disco ball that hangs near. If you're lucky, you'll catch a DJ spinning vinyl, taking requests and turning "let's just grab pizza" into a memorable evening. And, oh, if your brother's girlfriend is gluten-free (like I am), she can indulge, too: Kim developed a gluten-free crust that can stand up to the oven's 800°F heat. Produced off-site in a gluten-free facility and baked on a special pan, it offers a delightfully crispy chew to us otherwise pizza-deprived souls.

In case you're not completely stuffed with pies like the fried-egg-topped beauty known as The Sunnyside, there are soft-serve sundaes for dessert, drizzled with extra-virgin olive oil and topped with sea salt. Paired with chocolate chip cookies warmed in the pizza oven until fragrant and gooey, you might actually consider dropping by just for dessert. Except that would be silly.

Pizzeria Lola's best-selling pie represents all that has changed in Minneapolis–St. Paul dining in the last decade. In (what was) the land of not-too-spicy pepperoni, it is the Lady ZaZa that now rules supreme, topped with house-made kimchee and Korean sausage, serrano peppers, scallions, and a sesame-and-soy chili glaze. One could easily argue that the best Korean flavors in the Twin Cities are, in fact, at Pizzeria Lola. (Before I declare the end of pepperoni pizza in Minnesota, by the way, which is in fact my personal favorite, particularly at Lola where the natural-casing pepperoni bakes into glorious little cups of pork fat, I should also mention that the second best-selling pie is the My Sha-Roni. Topped with house red sauce, mozzarella, pepperoni, and house-made fennel sausage, it is of course a meaty classic.)

For Kim, a Korean immigrant who quit her day job as a law-school-trained theater actor to pursue her pizza passion, Pizzeria Lola is all about sharing food with others. "To me, food nourishes the body, but more importantly the soul. I love the communal aspect of food and how it brings people together. Plus, I get to make and eat pizza every day. It doesn't get any better than that."

CHEF ANN KIM'S MAKE-AT-HOME PIZZA DOUGH

(MAKES SIX 6-OUNCE, 10-INCH CRUSTS OR FOUR 9-OUNCE, 12-INCH CRUSTS)

Note: Prepare the dough the day before you plan to make and serve pizzas.

4¼ cups (23 ounces) bread flour, plus more as needed
1 teaspoon (0.1 ounce) instant yeast
2 cups (15 ounces) cold water, divided
3 teaspoons (0.3 ounces) kosher salt
Olive oil
Your favorite sauce, cheese, and toppings

In the bowl of a stand mixer with a dough hook, combine the flour and yeast. Add 1¾ cups of the water (reserving ¼ cup to add if necessary) and mix with dough hook attachment on low speed for 1 minute. Add salt and continue to mix for another 3 minutes, adding reserved water if the dough seems dry. Let the dough rest for 10 minutes, then mix again on medium-low speed for an additional 2 minutes, or until the dough no longer sticks to the side of the bowl. The dough should still be tacky to the touch, but not so wet and sticky that it does not hold its shape. If the dough is still too dry, slowly add water, 1 tablespoon at a time. If it is too wet, gradually mix in flour by the tablespoon until you reach the desired consistency. Do not overmix the dough.

Transfer the dough to a well-floured surface and gently pat the dough into a ball. Using a sharp knife, cut dough into six 6-ounce or four 9-ounce pieces and form each one into a tight ball. Place the dough balls on a baking sheet brushed with olive oil to prevent sticking. Brush dough balls with additional olive oil. Cover the dough balls with plastic wrap and let sit at room temperature for 30 minutes. Immediately place the dough balls in the refrigerator and let rest for 24 hours.

The next day, remove the dough balls and let sit at room temperature for 1–2 hours prior to making pizzas.

While dough rests at room temperature, set a baking stone in the center of oven and preheat the oven to 500°F, or as high as your oven will go, for a minimum of 1 hour.

When the oven is preheated, generously flour a pizza peel and set aside. Stretch the dough by hand, or by rolling with a rolling pin, to desired size and shape. Settle the crust onto the pizza peel, making sure the crust can slide around. Add more flour as necessary to keep the dough from sticking to the peel. Working quickly, top dough with your favorite sauce, cheese, and toppings.

Slide the pizza off the peel and onto the pizza stone. Cook for 6–7 minutes or until the crust is lightly browned and cheese has started to bubble and melt, being careful not to overbake, which is easy to do when oven temperatures are so high. Baking time will vary depending on the oven and preference for crispness.

Remove pizza with pizza peel to a cutting board. Slice and serve immediately.

THE RABBIT HOLE/
THE LEFT-HANDED COOK

920 E. Lake Street, Suite 101
Minneapolis, MN 55407
(612) 236-4526
EATDRINKRABBIT.COM
Co-Owners: Thomas Kim and Kat Melgaard
Executive Chef: Thomas Kim

After serving time in several of the top kitchens in Los Angeles and San Francisco, Thomas Kim agreed with his (then) girlfriend Kat Melgaard that it was time for a big change. The two packed up and headed for the land of The Replacements, Prince, and endless winters. Melgaard grew up in North Dakota, so she had an idea of what lay ahead weather-wise, but not much could have braced Minneapolis for their inventive Korean-fusion cuisine and searing sense of style. Inside their restaurant The Rabbit Hole, diners are dazzled by Melgaard's mind-blowing Lewis Carroll–esque decor, featuring

private dark-wood booths, arches of books that spiral through the air, tables that tumble down the walls while balancing teacups, and a chandelier that floats like a cloud of paper lanterns over the bar. Definitely visit their website for a delicious sense of what's in store upon your physical arrival.

Equally inventive are Kim's marvelously addictive dishes, with creative twists on Korean and American comfort-food classics. Plates of Duck, Duck, Dduk (rice cake with duck confit and *gochujang*), kimchee fried rice with bacon and a soft-poached egg, and all of The Rabbit Hole's burgers are crowd favorites. Add a sparkling craft cocktail and you have a smash hit, my friends, an unlikely hot spot given its tucked-away location in Midtown Global Market, but somehow it all works. Not only has their kimchee-spiked cuisine drawn rave reviews, but Twin Cities seem to have been good to these two as well. Since their arrival and restaurant opening, they've married and given birth to a beautiful little girl, making the move to Minneapolis more than a crazy (very busy!) dream, because now it's home.

The Rabbit Hole's Charred Green Beans with Garlic Black Bean Sauce

(SERVES 2–3)

Chef Kim's note: Items marked with an asterisk below can be found at Asian markets.

For the garlic black bean sauce:

½ cup grapeseed oil, divided

¼ cup roughly chopped whole fermented black beans*

¼ cup minced garlic

¼ cup minced ginger

1 bunch scallions, white and green parts, sliced ⅛-inch thick

2 teaspoon sambal (Thai chili sauce)*

¼ cup soju (Korean distilled liquor)*

1 teaspoon kosher salt

½ teaspoon ground black pepper

For the orange zest salt:

½ cup kosher salt

1½ tablespoons orange zest

½ tablespoon orange juice

For the green beans:

1 tablespoon slivered almonds

2 tablespoons grapeseed oil, divided

½ large onion, sliced thin

6 ounces green beans, trimmed

Jalapeño or white vinegar

1½ tablespoons garlic black bean sauce (see directions)

Pinch of orange zest salt

To make the garlic black bean sauce: Place a 12-inch skillet over medium heat. Add ¼ cup oil, black beans, garlic, ginger, and scallions. Sauté until al dente, about 10 minutes. Add sambal and soju. Season with salt and pepper and let cool.

Transfer two-thirds of mixture to the bowl of a blender and process until smooth. Add the remaining ¼ cup oil and process until emulsified. Scrape mixture into a small bowl and stir in remaining beans. Cover and store leftover bean sauce in the refrigerator indefinitely.

To make the orange zest salt: In a medium bowl, stir all ingredients together. Spread mixture on a parchment-paper-lined baking sheet and allow to dry for at least 4 hours. Crumble and store in a covered jar.

To make the green beans: Heat a 12-inch skillet over low heat. When pan is hot, add the almonds and, stirring frequently, toast until golden brown. Transfer to a small plate and set aside. Return pan to heat.

Turn heat to medium-low and add 1 tablespoon oil. When oil is hot, add onions and stir to coat with oil. Cook onions slowly, stirring often, until they are very soft and caramelized, about 20 minutes. Scrape them into a small bowl and set aside. Return pan to heat.

Turn heat to high and when pan is very hot, add remaining 1 tablespoon oil to the pan. When oil is shimmering hot, carefully add green beans to the pan. Char beans until one side has started to blacken in spots, then add the jalapeño vinegar. Toss beans while they steam in the vinegar, about 3 minutes. Add 2 tablespoons caramelized onions and cook until onions are warmed through. Stir in 1½ tablespoons garlic black bean sauce until the green beans are coated.

To serve: Plate the beans and garnish with orange zest salt and almonds.

THE LEFT-HANDED COOK'S H&K POUTINE

(SERVES 2–3)

For the pork belly curry:

½ cup curry mix (S&B or House Foods brand curries are good, available at Asian markets)

1½ cups pork belly braising liquid (or chicken stock)

1 cup braised pork belly pieces, chopped coarsely (any protein works well in this recipe; try tofu for a vegetarian version)

For the poutine:

2 tablespoon grapeseed oil, divided

½ large onion, sliced thin

1 tablespoon kimchee

7 ounces frozen french fries

4 ounces pork belly curry (see directions below)

1 large egg

1 tablespoon grated cheddar cheese

1 tablespoon grated Parmesan

To make the pork belly curry: In a small bowl, stir together curry mix and braising liquid until no lumps remain. The sauce should have the consistency of a thick gravy; add water if necessary for the desired consistency. Stir in pork belly pieces.

To make the poutine: In a 10-inch skillet over medium-low heat, add 1 tablespoon oil. When oil is hot, add onions and stir to coat with oil. Cook onions slowly, stirring often, until they are very soft and caramelized, about 20 minutes. Add kimchee and keep warm.

Bake fries according to package directions.

While fries cook, in a small saucepan, warm pork belly curry.

Set a small skillet over medium-high heat. Add remaining oil and, when hot, fry egg to desired doneness.

When fries are done, arrange them in a shallow bowl. Working quickly, top hot fries with cheeses and the onion-kimchee mixture, then pour the hot pork belly curry over everything. Top with the fried egg. Dig. In.

Rainbow Chinese Restaurant

2739 Nicollet Avenue
Minneapolis, MN 55408
(612) 870-7084
RAINBOWRESTAURANT.COM
Owner and Executive Chef: Tammy Wong

The irrepressible Tammy Wong is one of the Twin Cities' most-recognized chefs. She can be spotted almost every summer day at the Minneapolis Farmers' Market, chatting with the local growers who adore her, looking all of thirty years old, even though that's not possible because her restaurant, Rainbow Chinese, was founded in 1987.

"I have always loved to talk to people about their cuisines and to share stories, especially with people from different parts of the world. Hearing about and tasting how other people approach food and what their traditions are have always inspired me to keep cooking."

She integrates and generously passes along what she learns, whether she's cooking on the fly in front of a crowd or television audience or designing a menu for a catering client. I've watched several of her demos at the Minneapolis Farmers' Market—I consider

them a free class on "How to Have an Audience Eat Out of the Palm of Your Hand"—and particularly enjoy the way she uses charm and humor to cajole the most stubborn meat-and-potatoes dudes to try fresh vegetables. The verdict, every time? "This is delicious!" Wong laughs, says thank you, and stays late to answer cooking questions and offer encouragement for market goers to talk with the growers and to try new things. She encourages home cooks to learn to love a wide variety of vegetables by cooking simply with the freshest possible ingredients.

Over the last twenty-five years, Rainbow Chinese—the anchor of Nicollet Avenue's "Eat Street"—has launched chefs and bartenders into successful careers all over town. When I ask Wong if she feels like a mother hen, seeing her chicks venture out into the world, she chuckles and says that she does indeed enjoy keeping tabs on where they land and how they're doing, because to her, Rainbow Chinese is as much about people as it is about food.

"There are many things that I really love about running Rainbow. I love to cook, of course, I have always loved to cook. But getting a chance to interact and share a little bit about myself through my food with so many different people, as they come into the restaurant, is so energizing for me."

Steamed Fish with Ginger & Scallions

(SERVES 4)

1 (1½-pound) whole fresh fish, cleaned (walleye is Tammy's favorite, but sole and trout work as well)

⅓ cup soy sauce

4 tablespoons water

2 teaspoons sugar

3 inches fresh gingerroot, peeled and julienned

¼ cup julienned scallions (from 4–6 stalks)

Several dashes toasted sesame oil

2 tablespoons vegetable oil

Place a steamer basket over a 12-quart stockpot (or any stockpot that accommodates your steamer basket) with a lid. Fill the pot with water, stopping ½ inch below the steamer basket.

Set the pot over high heat and bring water to a boil. Place the fish in the steamer basket and cover. Steam the fish for 10–12 minutes or until it is cooked through. (To check fish, cut a small slit into the thickest portion; if the meat pulls easily from the bone, it's done.)

While the fish is steaming, in a small bowl whisk together the soy sauce, water, and sugar. Set aside.

When fish is done, use two spatulas to transfer it to a serving platter. Pour the soy sauce mixture over the fish, then evenly top with the ginger and scallions. Drizzle dashes of sesame oil over the ginger and scallions.

In a small saucepan, heat the vegetable oil over high heat until it just starts to smoke. Carefully and quickly pour the hot oil evenly over the fish (be aware that it will splatter and sizzle when it hits the ginger and scallions). Serve immediately.

Red Table Meats

1401 Marshall Street Northeast
Suite 100
Minneapolis, MN 55413
(612) 200-8245
redtablemeatco.com
Co-owner/Executive Chef: Michael Phillips

It's fair to say that Executive Chef Mike Phillips, aka the King of Meat, is one of the best-loved chefs in the Twin Cities. He's far too humble—and busy—to stand still long enough for anyone to compliment him, but he's made it his life's work to learn and generously share his knowledge about the great culinary art of *salumi* (dry-cured pork). Minnesota chefs and diners are forever grateful to have been along for the ride (that's a pun, by the way, as Phillips is an avid bicyclist).

And, oh, what a long ride it's been. Phillips left his job as executive chef of The Craftsman in Minneapolis in 2010 to start Green Ox Meat Company with business partner and local restaurateur Kieran Folliard. After false starts on finding a building in which to base the operation, complex zoning and certification puzzles to solve, and a couple of name changes to boot, the company is now Red Table Meat Company, and it is open for business. Hurrah! Our greasy little fingertips could not be happier.

It's important to note that for Phillips, the integrity of the pork is as important as the craft. He is a long-time advocate and supporter of small, sustainable farms. Red Table defines itself as a "for-benefit" company, with the goal of participating in and collaborating

with a community of farmers, butchers, and consumers "who are committed to sustainability and caring for the food system and who believe in taste as a testament to that commitment."

Phillips shares his message of sustainability plus craft widely, with other chefs who study with him to improve their own charcuterie-making skills, and with wildly popular whole-hog butchery classes at Kitchen in the Market. While it bewilders him that home cooks are so fascinated by the process of breaking down a pig, it's not hard to imagine why we all enjoy witnessing a master at work—art is art. Plus, everyone goes home with the best freshly made breakfast sausage on the planet.

CHARCUTERIE BREAD SALAD

(SERVES 6)

Chef Phillips's note: This is a perfect summer-harvest, use-up-your-old-bread-and-charcuterie-ends type of meal, very flexible. Make it with whatever you have on hand.

½ cup diced pancetta or guanciale

½ pound organic unsalted butter, divided

½ cup olive oil, divided

2 pounds old bread ends or crusty loaves, cut into 1-inch pieces

1 medium yellow onion, halved and sliced into ¼-inch slices

2 cloves garlic, chopped

3 cups vegetables (such as kohlrabi, snap peas, green beans), cut into 1-inch pieces

1 cup chopped salami or other charcuterie ends (coppa, pâté, etc.)

4 cups greens (such as chard, mustard, kale, rapini, kohlrabi greens), sliced into 1-inch-wide ribbons

2 cups cherry tomatoes

Salt and freshly ground pepper

Optional garnishes:

Chopped fresh herbs

Grated cheese

Poached eggs

Set a 14-inch skillet over medium heat. Add the pancetta and sauté until browned. Add half the butter and half the olive oil to the pan, then add the bread, vegetables (except the greens and tomatoes), and salami. Stir everything once to coat with oil, then don't stir again until the bread is browning nicely. Add more butter and oil as needed to keep the mixture from being dry. Turn occasionally until all the bread is browned.

Stir in the greens, which will stop the browning and steam things a bit. Add the cherry tomatoes to warm them through. Season with salt and pepper and top as you like with herbs, cheese, and/or eggs.

THE CO-OP GROCERY STORE MOVEMENT

The Twin Cities are blessed with a wide variety of food shopping options, from carpeted grocery stores lit by chandeliers to specialty food stores and seasonal farmers' markets. In the middle of the pack is an actively growing cooperative (co-op) shopping movement, one of the most vibrant in the country. What began in the 1970s with a handful of members collaboratively buying natural foods in bulk has grown into twelve sophisticated storefronts selling locally grown, locally produced, organic, pastured, and non-GMO (genetically modified organism) food to both of the Twin Cities and their surrounding suburbs.

And more—all co-ops are guided by seven common principles: voluntary and open membership; democratic member control; member economic participation; autonomy and independence; education, training, and information; cooperation among cooperatives; and concern for the community. For the neighborhoods that surround the co-ops, those principles translate to farm-fresh food *and* important programs, created with and for the neighborhoods and communities where the co-ops do business.

St. Paul's Mississippi Market's Limited-Income Membership Entry (LIME) initiative provides discounted co-op memberships to people in financial need, and its "Shopping on a Budget" course is so popular that co-ops around the country are using the curriculum in their stores. In 1994, Mississippi Market and Minneapolis's The Wedge Community Co-op cofounded Midwest Food Connection, a program that presents lessons about food and farming to thousands of area schoolchildren. The program is still going strong, with a team of educators working with public schools to introduce children to fresh food. As part of The Wedge's continued growth and expansion, they established Co-op Partners Warehouse in 1999, now a distributor of organic produce in six states, and started their own farm to meet their ever-growing demand for organic produce.

Seward Community Co-op has outgrown not one but two facilities and is continuing to expand. They offer one of the best meat counters in the Twin Cities, as well as cooking, health, lifestyle, parenting, and shopping classes for members and the community, and a popular community supported agriculture (CSA) fair each spring. Like Seward, Linden Hills Co-op outgrew its original home and took up residence in a former grocery store. Situated next to a garden center and across the street from one of the best wine shops in Minneapolis, they exemplify "heart-of-the-neighborhood" status.

From high-integrity, best-quality food to community partnership, education, environmental sustainability, and supporting local economies, the future is bright for the Twin Cities' co-op movement. See the National Cooperative Grocers Association website at strongertogether.coop for a comprehensive list of Minnesota co-ops.

Seward Community Co-op, Minneapolis

Spring CSA Box Pizza

(SERVES 4)

1 bunch asparagus, woody ends snapped off, sliced lengthwise into 1-inch pieces

4 petit pan or sunburst (pattypan) summer squashes, sliced thin

¾ pound sliced wild or farmed fresh mushrooms

2 tablespoons olive oil, plus more as needed

4 lavash breads (Holy Land brand preferred) or flatbread naans

1 pound fresh mozzarella, sliced as thin as possible

1 (4-ounce) log fresh chèvre (Stickney Hill preferred), broken into small ½- to ¼-inch pieces

1 large spring onion, bulb and green part sliced thin

2 tablespoons shredded Parmesan cheese

1 tablespoons fresh thyme leaves

Sea salt and freshly ground black pepper

Preheat oven to 450°F. If using a pizza stone, preheat that in the oven, too. (Otherwise you can place individual pizzas directly on the center rack.)

Lightly sauté asparagus, summer squash, and mushrooms separately, but in the same pan, using 2 tablespoons oil in batches. Use more oil if needed. Set each vegetable aside separately in small bowls as you go.

Lay out the 4 lavash breads on a board or on the counter. Divide and distribute the mozzarella cheese among them all. Distribute all the other sautéed vegetables evenly among the pizzas on top of the mozzarella cheese.

Divide and distribute the chèvre pieces with your fingers evenly among each pizza. This is kind of messy as the cheese is a bit wet and sticky.

Sprinkle the spring onions around the pizzas, followed by the Parmesan cheese and fresh thyme. Season with salt and pepper.

Bake pizzas for 15–18 minutes, or until crust is golden brown.

Serve with a side salad . . . some of the ingredients of which you may find in the very same CSA box!

PREMIUM ROTISSERIE

BRASA

ORGANIC · LOCAL · NATURAL

Restaurant Alma/Brasa Premium Rotisserie

528 University Ave Southeast
Minneapolis, MN 55414
(612) 379-4909
www.restaurantalma.com

Brasa Premium Rotisserie
600 E. Hennepin Avenue
Minneapolis, MN 55414
(612) 379-3030

777 Grand Avenue
St. Paul, MN 55105
(651) 224-1302
www.brasa.us
Chef/Owner: Alexander Roberts

Opening a Creole-influenced restaurant using locally sourced, sustainably raised ingredients might not be the logical next step for a fine-dining-trained, James Beard Award–winning chef, but that is exactly what Chef Alex Roberts did—twice! His flagship, Restaurant Alma, has long romanced fans with its beautiful candle-lit dining room, exquisite wine list, and flawlessly executed food. The menu changes every couple of months, but always includes starters, grains and pastas, and meats and fish with which to build a luxurious-yet-affordable three-course dinner, which in effect makes Restaurant Alma date-night heaven. Whether you're a long-married couple treating yourselves on a weeknight or a new pair in the throes of mad love, this is food made for seduction. That said, I've had beautiful meals sitting alone at the bar, sipping wine and chatting with the top-notch staff. Whether you're a group of one or twelve, just know that Alma is one of Minneapolis's finest restaurants—it is a treasure.

Brasa, located in both Minneapolis and St. Paul, is much more casual, with garage doors that roll open on warm summer days to reveal jovial tables of friends and plenty of families (the children's menu is delightful). Brasa's specialty is succulent, slow-roasted meats—pork shoulder, rotisserie chicken, and smoked beef—piled into sandwiches or sold by weight to carry out with craveable sides like crispy yucca, yellow rice and beans (red, black, pigeon peas, and sometimes black-eyed peas with bacon, which are insanely delicious, so order them if you luck into them), smoky collard greens, or fresh-fried tortilla chips and guacamole. Highly executed, best-quality comfort food is a winning formula (take note!), and as a result, Brasa is hoppin' all day and night. As a bonus, gluten-free diners have almost the entire menu to choose from, a fact that has cemented a deep and loyal following in the food-allergy community. I myself have been known to sit in my car, in the parking lot, digging into the food I was supposed to be carrying home. . . .

Restaurant Alma's Ricotta Gnocchi with Lobster, Truffle Butter & Orange

(SERVES 8 GENEROUSLY)

For the dried orange powder:

2 oranges, zested and segmented, segments cut into
    1-inch pieces

For the gnocchi:

2½ pounds whole milk ricotta cheese
2 ounces Parmigiano Reggiano cheese, grated
10 large organic eggs
5 large organic egg yolks
4 cups all-purpose flour
Salt and freshly ground pepper
Olive oil

For the lobster and lobster stock:

2 (1½-pound) lobsters
2 tablespoons minced celery
2 tablespoons minced carrot
2 tablespoons minced onion
1 sprig fresh parsley
1 sprig fresh thyme
4 peppercorns
1 bay leaf

For the truffle-lobster butter:

1 tablespoon heavy cream
½ pound cold unsalted butter, diced
1 teaspoon minced black truffle shavings
Drizzle of truffle oil
Lemon half
Salt and freshly ground pepper

For the garnish:

¼ cup minced chives

To make the dried orange powder: Preheat oven to 135°F. Spread orange zest on a parchment-paper-lined baking sheet. Bake zest until completely dry, 3–4 hours. Cool for a few minutes then grind to a powder in spice grinder. Reserve for garnish.

To make the gnocchi: In the bowl of a stand mixer, combine ricotta, Parmigiano Reggiano, eggs, egg yolks, flour, 1 teaspoon salt, and a few grinds of pepper. Mix on low speed until just combined (do not overmix).

Transfer dough to a pastry bag (or plastic bag with corner snipped away). Bring a large pot of salted water to a boil, then turn heat to low so water is simmering. Set out a baking sheet and brush lightly with olive oil. Working over the water, squeeze 1 x 1-inch pieces of dough from the bag and, using a paring knife, trim so dough pieces fall into the water. Continue until all dough has been used. Allow gnocchi to float for 1–2 minutes before removing with a slotted spoon and transferring to baking sheet. When all the gnocchi are cooked, place baking sheet in refrigerator and allow to cool completely.

For the lobster: Set a medium saucepan of salted water over high heat and bring to a boil. Set out a large bowl of ice water. Remove claws and tail from lobsters (reserve bodies). Boil claws for 7 minutes and tails for 5 minutes, immersing both claws and tails immediately in ice water to stop the cooking process.

Clean the meat from the shells and dice meat into small bite-size pieces; discard shells. Cover and chill.

To make the lobster stock: Crush the lobster bodies with a rolling pin or meat hammer and place in a medium saucepan. Add a splash of water to the pan and set over medium heat. When water is steaming, cover pot, turn heat to low, and steam lobster bodies gently for 15 minutes.

Uncover pot and add celery, carrot, onion, parsley, thyme, peppercorns, bay leaf, and water to cover. Bring to boil, turn heat to low, and simmer uncovered for 45–60 minutes. Strain broth through fine chinois lined with cheesecloth into a large bowl; discard lobster bodies. Cool completely.

For the truffle-lobster butter: Pour half of the lobster stock into a small saucepan. Set over medium heat and bring to a boil. Reduce stock until almost dry—leaving about 2 tablespoons in the pan—remove pan from heat, and add the heavy cream and butter. Stir constantly until emulsified and smooth.

Stir in the black truffle shavings, black truffle oil, and a small squeeze of lemon juice. Keep in a warm (not hot) place until ready to serve.

To serve: In a saucepan large enough to hold the truffle butter, lobster, and gnocchi, over low heat gently warm poached lobster and cooked gnocchi in the truffle butter along with a little reserved lobster stock. Take care not to overheat the butter or you'll break the emulsification or overcook the lobster. Divide gnocchi among warm bowls. Season with salt and pepper to taste. Garnish with 4 or 5 orange pieces, orange powder, and chives.

Brasa's Pork Shoulder Roasted with Citrus Mojo

(SERVES 8)

Note: The roast can be made up to two days ahead. Cool, cover, and refrigerate whole. Bring to room temperature and then shred. Cover and reheat gently at 300°F until warmed through.

1 tablespoon extra-virgin olive oil

½ cup minced onion

2 large garlic cloves, minced

1 cup fresh lemon juice

1 cup fresh orange juice

2 tablespoons distilled white vinegar

2 tablespoons garlic powder

2 tablespoons onion powder

2 tablespoons freshly ground pepper, plus more as needed

1½ teaspoons ground cumin

1 tablespoon Worcestershire sauce

Salt

1 (5-pound) bone-in Boston butt (pork shoulder, butt end)

In a small saucepan, heat the olive oil over medium heat. Add the onion and cook until softened, about 5 minutes. Add the garlic and cook until fragrant, about 2 minutes. Add the lemon and orange juices and simmer for 2 minutes. Stir in the vinegar. Transfer half of the mojo to a blender and let cool. Refrigerate the remaining mojo.

Meanwhile, in a jar, shake together the garlic and onion powders, pepper, and cumin. Add 2 tablespoons of this dry rub to the mojo in the blender; reserve remaining rub. Add Worcestershire and 1 tablespoon salt to the blender and puree mojo until smooth.

Put the pork in a sealable 1-gallon plastic bag and pour in the marinade. Press as much air as you can from the bag and seal. Refrigerate pork for at least 8 hours and up to 24 hours, turning occasionally. Bring the pork to room temperature before roasting.

Preheat oven to 350°F and set a rack in a roasting pan large enough to hold the pork. Remove the pork from the marinade and pat dry with paper towels. Rub the meat all over with the remaining dry rub and transfer pork to the rack. Roast pork for 3 hours, or until an instant-read thermometer inserted into the thickest part of the meat registers 150°F. Reduce the oven temperature to 275°F and roast the meat for approximately 3 hours longer, until very tender and an instant-read thermometer reads 180°F. Remove the roast from the oven and cover with foil; let rest for 30 minutes.

Shred the meat, discarding the bones and excess fat. Season pork with salt and pepper and serve with the remaining mojo.

Saffron Restaurant & Lounge/ World Street Kitchen

123 N. 3rd Street
Minneapolis, MN 55401
(612) 746-5533
SAFFRONMPLS.COM

World Street Kitchen
2743 Lyndale Avenue South
Minneapolis, MN 55408
(612) 424-8855
EATWSK.COM
Co-Owner: Saed Wadi
Co-Owner/Executive Chef: Sameh Wadi

I suspect that if Sameh Wadi weren't a chef, he could make his living as a storyteller. It helps that his personal story packs three lifetimes into his thirty years, but add the sparking energy, bawdy laugh, and quick wit, and I'm telling you, he may have missed his calling.

Or not. Wadi is a successful, award-winning chef, and the Twin Cities food scene would be a different—and less delicious place—without him.

Born in Kuwait to Palestinian parents, Wadi was raised in Jordan in a seriously food-focused home. "My parents wrote a cookbook in the late 1980s. My mother was always an amazing cook; every day was a Thanksgiving-like feast. I shadowed my mother in her kitchen from a very young age; she taught me the basics and the appreciation for food."

Wadi was thirteen years old when he moved to the Twin Cities in 1997. He spent the summer working in his family's grocery store in south Minneapolis, where he developed an impression of the Twin Cities as a diverse community. When school started and he showed up for his first day at suburban Irondale High School, he was stunned by the sea of white faces. After having to explain to students that he wasn't Mexican, Wadi made his way through high school on equal parts humor, toughness, and his love of food and cooking.

After high school, Wadi enrolled in the Art Institutes International culinary program in Minneapolis. Even while he was in school, influenced by his family's recipes and then-Solera chef and mentor Tim McKee, Wadi was dreaming of opening his own Mediterranean-inspired restaurant. In 2007, at the age of twenty-three, he and his brother Saed opened Saffron and made the dream a reality. With beautifully executed, creative takes on Middle Eastern and Mediterranean classics, Saffron has been well-received since the day it opened. While the kitchen turns out dishes like Moroccan duck *kefta* tagine and whole roasted branzini with crispy grape leaves, Saffron's bar program pours gorgeous cocktails crafted by award-winning bartender Robert Jones. There is no more romantic date night than an evening spent at Saffron's warmly lit bar, sipping drinks and sharing mezes.

Saffron
RESTAURANT & LOUNGE

Despite the restaurant's success, it's a little bit easy to forget that Saffron is Executive Chef Wadi's flagship. Just a few years after opening Saffron, the brothers launched their World Street Kitchen food truck, which won fast fans for big-flavor favorites like the Bangkok Burrito and Yum Yum Rice Bowl. An uptown Minneapolis brick-and-mortar World Street Kitchen storefront followed in 2012, adding brunch and home delivery to the mix in 2013.

Executive Chef Wadi himself gained a large personal following after competing on the Food Network's *Iron Chef America* in 2010, almost defeating Iron Chef Masaharu Morimoto. He has been nominated as both a James Beard Foundation Rising Star Chef and Best Chef Midwest Semifinalist. In 2009, he launched Spice Trail, a line of blended spices available for purchase at Saffron.

As much as he enjoys working with food, in the end it's about connecting with people. "The most enjoyable part of being a chef and a restaurateur is easily the people that you meet and the memories that you make with them."

SAFFRON'S GRILLED LAMB CHOPS WITH GREEK SPICE & HERBS

(SERVES 4)

For the Greek spice (makes ¾ cup):

5 tablespoons black peppercorns
1 tablespoon green peppercorns
1½ teaspoons whole coriander seeds
1 tablespoon dried oregano
5 teaspoons garlic powder
2 tablespoons citric acid

For the lamb chops:

4 tablespoons olive oil, divided
1 (4-pound or approximately 8-bone) rack of lamb, chine
   bone removed, fat cap trimmed, rack cut into chops
Greek spice (see recipe)
4 fresh oregano sprigs
4 fresh thyme sprigs
2 whole lemons, sliced
Sea salt

To make the Greek spice: In a dry 10-inch skillet over medium heat, toast black peppercorns, green peppercorns, and coriander until fragrant. Cool.

In a spice or coffee grinder, grind together the toasted spices and oregano to a fine powder. Transfer to a small bowl and add garlic powder and citric acid. Mix thoroughly. Store any unused spice in an airtight container at room temperature.

To make the lamb chops: Drizzle 2 tablespoons olive oil on a baking sheet. Arrange the lamb chops over the oil and drizzle remaining oil over chops. Turn chops to coat evenly in oil, then sprinkle generously on both sides with Greek spice (you will not use all of the Greek spice). Transfer seasoned chops to a heavy-duty freezer bag, add the fresh herb sprigs and lemon slices, and seal. Refrigerate for a minimum of 2 hours and up to overnight.

Preheat charcoal or gas grill until very hot. While grill heats, remove chops from refrigerator and bring to room temperature. Remove chops from bag, discarding bag with herbs and lemon, and season chops with salt. Grill chops over high heat to desired doneness (time will vary depending on grill and cut of chops, usually around 3½ minutes per side for medium; the spice blend helps to achieve a crusty-charred exterior).

Let chops rest on a cutting board for 5 minutes before serving with farrotto and brussels sprouts (see recipes that follow).

WINTER SQUASH FARROTTO

(SERVES 4–6)

2 cups farro

3½ cups water

2½ tablespoons sea salt divided, plus more to taste

½ cup extra-virgin olive oil

1 large butternut squash, peeled, halved lengthwise,
  seeds removed, and cut into 1-inch pieces

½ cup vegetable oil, divided

½ pound unsalted butter (2 sticks)

½ cup heavy cream, warmed

2 garlic cloves, sliced thin

2 cups vegetable stock

2 tablespoons finely chopped chives

Place farro in a colander and rinse well under running tap water. Add farro to a dutch oven or other large pot, then add water and 1½ tablespoons sea salt. Set uncovered pot over high heat and bring to a boil. Continue boiling for 5 minutes, then remove from heat and cover for 20 minutes (until farro is tender). Stir in olive oil and spread farro on a baking sheet. Refrigerate until cool.

Meanwhile, preheat oven to 400°F and line a baking sheet with parchment paper. In a large mixing bowl, toss squash with ¼ cup vegetable oil and 1 tablespoon sea salt. Spread squash on baking sheet and roast until very tender, about 20 minutes. Set squash aside to cool.

In a large saucepan, heat butter over medium heat. Butter will melt and then foam up. When the foam subsides and brown flecks start to appear, whisk the butter until it turns a rich brown color and has a nutty smell. Remove butter from heat and strain through a fine mesh strainer. Set aside.

Transfer 3 cups warm squash (leaving the rest on the baking sheet) to the bowl of a food processor and puree with butter and warm cream until smooth. Set aside.

Heat a 12-inch (or larger) skillet over medium-high heat. When the pan is hot, add the remaining ¼ cup vegetable oil and sauté garlic until fragrant, about 1 minute. Add roasted squash, farro, and vegetable stock to the pan and bring to a simmer. Stir in the squash puree and continue simmering until mixture is thick and creamy, about 5 minutes. Season to taste with sea salt and stir in chives to finish.

CHARRED BRUSSELS SPROUTS WITH BAGNA CAUDA

(SERVES 4–6)

For the bagna cauda (makes ½ cup):

3 ounces oil-packed anchovy fillets, rinsed (Scalia brand
preferred, if you can find it)
1 cup Italian parsley leaves
¼ pound unsalted butter (1 stick)
1 garlic clove, peeled and grated

For the brussels sprouts:

1–2 cups kosher salt
1 tablespoon baking soda
1½ pounds brussels sprouts, trimmed and halved
lengthwise
½ cup vegetable oil
¼ cup bagna cauda
¼ cup fresh lemon juice
2 tablespoons finely chopped chives

To make the bagna cauda: Place all ingredients
in food processor and puree until smooth. This
makes more than is needed for the brussels
sprouts recipe; cover and chill leftover butter, or
wrap and freeze for up to a month.

To make the brussel sprouts: Fill a large bowl with
ice water and set aside. Fill a dutch oven or other
large pot with water. Season water with enough
salt "to taste like the ocean." (If you don't know
what the ocean tastes like, put this book down,
book a ticket to the nearest beach, jump into the
water, enjoy swimming, then return and get back
to cooking). Add baking soda and bring to a boil.

Blanch brussels sprouts in boiling water until just
tender, about 5 minutes. Drain in a colander and
transfer sprouts immediately to ice bath to halt
cooking. When sprouts are cooled, after 3–4
minutes, drain once again in colander.

Heat oil in a 12-inch (or larger) sauté pan over
high heat until oil is very hot and starts to smoke.
Carefully add brussels sprouts, cut side down,
and cook until browned, about 5 minutes. Add
bagna cauda, turn heat to low, and continue
cooking until butter melts. Add the lemon juice
and chives, stir to coat the sprouts, and season
with salt, if needed.

WORLD STREET KITCHEN'S ALOO TIKKI

(MAKES 6 PATTIES)

Sea salt

2 large russet potatoes, peeled

¼ cup chana dal (yellow split peas)

1 cup water

2 teaspoons black mustard seeds, toasted and ground

½ teaspoon black onion seeds, toasted and ground

½ tablespoon cumin seeds, toasted and ground

½ tablespoon coriander seeds, toasted and ground

⅛ teaspoon turmeric powder

¾ teaspoon cayenne powder

1½ teaspoons Spanish sweet smoked paprika

1 teaspoon garam masala (Spice Trail preferred)

1½ tablespoons minced jalapeño pepper

½ cup minced yellow onion

1 clove garlic, minced

1 teaspoon minced peeled fresh ginger

1 teaspoon lime juice

¼ cup vegetable oil

For the garnishes:

Fried rice noodles

Cilantro leaves

Chutney

Greek yogurt

Pomegranate seeds

Fill a large saucepan with cold, salted water. Add the potatoes and bring to a boil over high heat. Turn heat to low, cover pan, and cook potatoes until tender, about 20 minutes. Drain potatoes and chill uncovered in the refrigerator.

Rinse the chana dal in a colander under running tap water until water runs clear. Add the chana dal and 1 cup water to saucepan, bring to boil over high heat, turn heat to low, partially cover, and simmer until beans are almost tender, about 30 minutes. Remove pan from heat and stir in 1 teaspoon salt. Let beans sit until fully cooked but not mushy, about 20 minutes.

Shred cold potatoes on the coarse side of a box grater and transfer to a large bowl. Add spices, jalapeño, onion, garlic, ginger, lime juice, and cooked chana dal and mix thoroughly. Season to taste with salt. Form into six 3-ounce patties.

Heat oil in a 12-inch skillet over medium-high heat. When oil is hot, fry patties until browned and crispy on one side, about 4 minutes. Turn and cook until crispy on second side. Drain on paper towels. Serve hot with garnishes.

HEART BEATS COCKTAIL

Created by Robb Jones, Head Bartender, Saffron

(MAKES 1 DRINK)

For the red beet syrup:

2 beets, peeled
Granulated beet sugar

For the cocktail:

2 ounces gin (London Dry preferred)
0.75 ounce red beet syrup (above)
0.75 ounce fresh lemon juice
0.25 ounce dry orange curaçao
1 large egg white
Ice
Dash of absinthe
Peychaud's bitters

To make the beet syrup: Juice beets in a masticating juicer. Combine the volume of the juice with an equal part sugar and shake until combined. Shake it some more. Now shake it some more.

To make cocktail: Combine all ingredients except absinthe and bitters, and dry shake (shake without ice) to emulsify the egg. Add several good, thick chunks of ice and shake HARD. Rinse a chilled glass (preferably a coupe or cocktail glass) with the absinthe. Strain drink into glass.

Garnish with bitters heart. Enjoy!

SALTY TART

920 E. LAKE STREET
MINNEAPOLIS, MN 55407
(612) 874-9206
SALTYTART.COM
OWNER/EXECUTIVE CHEF: MICHELLE GAYER

"Force of nature" comes to mind when you find yourself in the presence of Executive Chef Michelle Gayer. She may spend the majority of her time in a cloud of sugar and pastry flour, but she's recognized all over the country for her award-winning crackling, crusty breads and ethereal pastries. And also for her infectious laugh: Gayer is charming, marvelously bawdy, smart as a whip, and highly unshy. Customers love to catch her in her shop because she's a blast to talk to and because in this town, she is a rock star. From working with the late, great Charlie Trotter in Chicago, to taking Minneapolis by buttercream storm, Gayer has been nominated as Best Pastry Chef and Best Chef Midwest twice over by the James Beard Foundation. Named Best Pastry Chef by *Bon Appétit* magazine, she's also been a featured chef at South Beach Wine and Food Festival, and the accolades continue to pour in. Her golden-domed milk buns have inspired a devoted following, and her coconut macaroons (aka crackaroons, which just happen to be gluten-free) were declared by friend Andrew Zimmern as his selection for *The Best Thing I Ever Ate* on the Food Network.

How best to indulge in a Salty Tart creation? The shop sits smack in the middle of Midtown Global Market on Lake Street in Minneapolis, so swing by to stock up on buttery cookies, tender brioche piped full of pastry cream, cupcakes piled high with icing, or a perfect baguette. Check out Salty Tart's stunning website for order-ahead inspiration (and dessert daydreaming). And if you find yourself at the Minnesota State Fair—and almost every Twin Citian does—make sure to track down the Salty Tart booth.

As if she weren't busy enough taking over the pastry world, Gayer has hosted Share Our Strength's annual Cakewalk fund-raiser for the last two years, a sugar-addict's wonderland of confections created by the Twin Cities' top pastry chefs. Partygoers ooh and ahh, sip cocktails, bid on their favorites, and cross their fingers that their bid comes out on top.

While Gayer worked with Charlie Trotter, the two coauthored a cookbook called *Charlie Trotter's Desserts*. I'll go out on a limb and say that there are plenty of fans in town waiting for a Salty Tart cookbook someday.

PLUM TART

(SERVES 8–10)

For the crust:

8 ounces browned unsalted butter (chilled until cold)
8 ounces cream cheese
8 ounces all-purpose flour
Salt

For the pastry cream:

1 large egg
2 large egg yolks
½ cup sugar, divided
3 tablespoons cornstarch
2 cups whole milk
1 vanilla bean, split lengthwise, insides scraped out, shell discarded (or 1 tablespoon pure vanilla extract)
2 tablespoons unsalted butter

For the almond cream:

3 ounces unsalted butter
⅓ cup sugar
1 large egg
1 large egg yolk

2 teaspoons vanilla extract
2 teaspoons grated lemon zest
3 tablespoons all-purpose flour
1 cup almond meal

For assembly:

All-purpose flour
3–4 red or black plums, thinly sliced
Egg wash (1 large egg beaten with 1 tablespoon water)
Sugar, for sprinkling
Honey, for garnish

To make the crust: Cut cold butter and cream cheese into ½- to 1-inch cubes. Place all ingredients in the bowl of a stand mixer and mix on low until just combined. There will still be large pieces of butter and cream cheese visible in the dough. Form into a ball, wrap in plastic, and chill dough for 3–4 hours.

To make the pastry cream: In a medium bowl, whisk egg, egg yolks, ¼ cup sugar, and cornstarch until smooth.

In a medium saucepan, heat milk, remaining ¼ cup sugar, and vanilla bean until milk just boils. Whisking the entire time, slowly add milk to the egg mixture. Pour pastry cream mixture back into pan and cook over medium heat, stirring constantly, until cream thickens and boils. Boil for 1 minute, then pull from heat. Press pastry cream through a mesh strainer into a medium bowl, then whisk in butter. Cover with plastic and chill until cold.

To make the almond cream: In the bowl of a stand mixer, cream butter and sugar together. With the mixer on medium speed, add the egg and when it's incorporated, add the egg yolk. Continue to mix on medium speed until smooth, about 3 minutes. Turn speed to low, add vanilla extract, lemon zest, flour, and almond meal, and mix until combined, about 2 minutes.

Scrape cold pastry cream into the almond cream and mix on low speed until combined, about 2 minutes. Set aside.

To assemble the tart: Preheat oven to 375°F. On a floured surface, roll chilled dough into an 11-inch circle, dusting with flour as needed to prevent sticking. Gently transfer dough to an 8-inch tart pan. Leave extra dough hanging over the side of the pan.

Fill tart three-quarters full with almond pastry cream. Lay plum slices in a slightly overlapping, concentric circle pattern, starting at the outer edge of the crust and working your way to the middle. Fold hanging crust up and over the top of the tart, crimping the edges. Brush egg wash over the crust edges and sprinkle generously with sugar.

Bake tart approximately 1 hour or until crust is golden. Brush warm tart with honey. Serve warm, or cool to room temperature.

SANCTUARY RESTAURANT

903 WASHINGTON AVENUE SOUTH
MINNEAPOLIS, MN 55415
(612) 339-5058
SANCTUARYMINNEAPOLIS.COM
OWNERS: MICHAEL KUTSCHEID, NAOMI WILLIAMSON,
    AND ROGER KUBICKI
EXECUTIVE CHEF: PATRICK ATANALIAN

There's a truth about Minnesotans: We're a bit unadventurous when it comes to food. Despite being the home state of eater extraordinaire Andrew Zimmern (he was raised in New York), we're late to the game of bold seasoning, fusion cuisine, and trusting a chef to lead us on a culinary adventure. Garrison Keillor would chalk it up to our Lutheran heritage, and while that's likely true, it's also true that palates are loosening up and diners are becoming braver, due in part to French-born Executive Chef Patrick Atanalian, aka Frenchie, who has been cooking at Sanctuary since 2008 (and at the Loring Cafe and New French Cafe before that).

Sanctuary's warm, funky, gargoyle-dotted interior is a perfect match for Atanalian's New American meets French meets Asian cuisine. With a firm grasp on classic French technique, Atanalian pushes familiar boundaries, guiding diners on delightful and unexpected culinary journeys made up of equal parts good humor and best-quality ingredients. With dishes like pan-seared barramundi in yuzu pao sauce with organic hazelnut chocolate risotto, watermelon radish, and English pea salad, Atanalian raises eyebrows and then delivers in style. It all fits for a chef who works with food "for the magic of cooking, of changing things. I love the transformation of the ingredients, the difference in smell, taste, color, and texture. And, it pays better than surfing."

In the summer and fall, Guthrie Theater fans can be found lounging on Sanctuary's romantic, secluded patio before and after the show, sipping wine and enjoying the stellar service—as friendly, fun, and professional as it gets in the Twin Cities. The only explanation for Sanctuary flying under the local food-award radar (their online customer ratings hover near perfect), is that before-mentioned, slowly thawing Minnesota palate. Atanalian's fiercely loyal fans know that Sanctuary is an affordable, delightful gem and that Frenchie is one-of-a-kind.

SALMON TARTARE

(SERVES 4)

1 pound sashimi-grade salmon, diced
½ teaspoon chopped garlic
2 tablespoons chopped scallions
1 tablespoon chopped fresh cilantro
1 tablespoon vegetable oil
1 tablespoon lime juice
Pinch of crushed red pepper flakes
Salt
1 cup cold heavy whipping cream
1 teaspoon wasabi powder
¼ cup Nutella

For garnish:

Wasabi peas
Pickled ginger

Place salmon in a large bowl and gently mix in garlic, scallions, cilantro, oil, lime juice, and red pepper flakes. Add salt to taste.

Whip heavy cream with wasabi powder. Add salt to taste.

Set out four salad plates. Using a pastry brush, paint a swath of Nutella across each plate. Use a 3-inch ring mold to shape tartare on each plate. Top with a dollop of whipped cream. Garnish with wasabi peas and pickled ginger. Enjoy!

Sea Change Restaurant & Bar

806 S. 2ND STREET
MINNEAPOLIS, MN 55415
(612) 225-6499
SEACHANGEMPLS.COM
OWNER: GUTHRIE THEATER
EXECUTIVE CHEF: TIM MCKEE
CHEF DE CUISINE: JAMIE MALONE

Opening a sustainable seafood restaurant in the middle of the country, in a landlocked state whose most famous (or infamous) fish dish is lutefisk (dried, reconstituted fish cured in lye), might have seemed like a long shot. But James Beard Award–winning Executive Chef Tim McKee thought otherwise—thank goodness. Since opening its doors in 2009 at the base of the stunning Guthrie Theater 2.0, Sea Change has won the hearts and stomachs of even the most jaded skeptics. It turns out that Twin Citians are crazy for top-quality, beautifully cooked fish, especially when prepared by one of the most talented young chefs in the country. Named in 2013 as one of *Food & Wine* magazine's Best New Chefs and in 2014 as a James Beard Foundation Semifinalist for Best Chef Midwest, Chef de Cuisine Malone (pictured) is quietly running one of the best sustainable seafood kitchens in the country. Her light touch and playful take on elegance set her apart from other Twin Cities chefs; both qualities shine through equally in fish dishes like crisp-skinned arctic char with white beans and artichoke giardiniera, and "not fish" dishes like cauliflower custard with crispy sweetbreads and cauliflower broth.

My favorite winter spot at Sea Change is at the raw bar, where Chef Holly Carson shucks oysters so elegantly and quickly that you can't stop watching. The silky Hawaiian ahi tuna poke is dreamy, as is the langoustine doused in searing-hot olive oil, chile, and rosemary. My favorite summer spot is on the patio, in the shadows of the Guthrie and Mill City ruins, facing one of the best views in all of Minnesota: the Mississippi River's St. Anthony Falls rushing under the historic Stone Arch Bridge. Make sure to take an after-dinner stroll along the riverfront for an evening you won't soon forget.

sea CHANGE
RESTAURANT & BAR

Chicken Breast with Country Ham, Velveeta Gratin & Collard Green Crisp

(SERVES 2)

Note: Begin this recipe the day before or morning of the day you plan to serve it.

For the crisps:

4 paper-thin slices country ham, sliced from frozen ham
Chicken skin from 2 chicken breasts
Kosher salt
Pinch of cayenne pepper
Oil for high-heat frying (safflower, peanut, or canola)
3 collard green leaves, center ribs removed, halved

For the Velveeta cheese sauce:

4 ounces Velveeta
4 ounces heavy whipping cream
4 ounces unsalted butter (1 stick)

For the Velveeta gratin:

2 medium russet potatoes, peeled and sliced very thinly
    with a mandoline
Velveeta cheese sauce (see above), warmed
½ cup cold unsalted butter (1 stick), cut into small dice
2 shallots, peeled, sliced ¼-inch thin, and separated
    into rings

For the chicken:

4 skin-on airline chicken breasts (boneless breast
    with drumette attached; call your butcher ahead to
    request)
Kosher salt
2 tablespoons vegetable oil

To make ham crisps: Turn the oven to 170°F. Line a baking sheet with parchment paper. Lay ham slices out flat on pan and bake for 3–4 hours, until ham is dry and crisp; or, dehydrate overnight in a dehydrator. Reserve at room temperature.

To make chicken crisps: Preheat oven to 225°F. Line a baking sheet with a silicone baking mat or parchment paper. Clean any fat from chicken skin, then lay skin out flat on pan. Cover with another sheet of parchment and rest three or four more baking sheets on top of the skin. Roast in the oven for 2 hours, or until crisp.

Season with salt and sprinkle lightly with cayenne pepper. Transfer to a rack to cool.

To make collard crisps: Preheat oven to 225°F. Line a baking sheet with parchment paper. Fill a large saucepan with 2 inches of vegetable oil. Heat oil over medium-high heat to 350°F. Fry one collard piece at a time until bubbling and dark green, 2–3 minutes. Transfer to baking sheet. Fry the remaining collard pieces, one at a time.

Season fried collard leaves with salt and bake until dry, about 30 minutes. Cool to room temperature.

To make Velveeta cheese sauce: In a small saucepan over low heat, combine all ingredients and stir until melted. Do not boil.

To make Velveeta gratin: Preheat oven to 350°F. Line a baking sheet with parchment paper. Lay 1 slice of potato on the baking sheet, brush with Velveeta cheese sauce. Shingle with another layer of potato, brush with cheese sauce, then top with a couple of pieces of butter and a couple of shallot rings. Continue, brushing with cheese sauce and adding butter and shallots every other layer, until potato stack is 2 inches high. Make a separate stack (or more) using the same process.

Top potatoes with a sheet of parchment paper, and then with another couple baking sheets to weigh the potatoes down. Bake potatoes for 1 hour or until easily pierced with a knife. Cool potatoes under weighted pans.

For the chicken breasts and to serve: Preheat oven to 375°F. Pat chicken dry with paper towels. Season breasts with kosher salt. Add oil to a 12-inch sauté pan and set over medium-high heat until oil is shimmering hot. Place chicken breasts skin side down in the pan and cook until the skin browns and releases from the pan, about 10 minutes.

Transfer chicken to a baking sheet, skin side up, and bake for 15 minutes or until chicken is cooked through. Transfer chicken breasts to a cutting board to rest for 10 minutes. Reheat potatoes while chicken rests.

To serve: Set out two warm, large, shallow bowls. Add chicken and potatoes to bowl and garnish with shards of crispy chicken skin, ham, and collard leaves.

Sen Yai Sen Lek

2422 Central Avenue Northeast
Minneapolis, MN 55418
(612) 781-3046
senyai-senlek.com
Co-Owner: Holly Hatch-Surisook
Co-Owner/Executive Chef: Joe Hatch-Surisook

In the winter, fragrance and color are in short supply in Minnesota, which makes Sen Yai Sen Lek all the more delightful. Both sit-down and take-out diners are drawn in by spicy, rich smells and, once inside, comforted by softly colored walls covered with an array of contemporary and traditional artwork, as well as warm Hatch-Surisook hospitality.

Executive Chef Joe Hatch-Surisook learned to cook traditional Thai dishes in his family's kitchen in Bangkok and later in Chicago. In Minneapolis, he cooked with Chef Michael Phillips, now of Red Table Meat Company, at Chet's Taverna, where they developed relationships with local farmers for top-notch produce and meat. As Hatch-Surisook and his wife, Holly, planned a restaurant of their own, they envisioned a cozy,

neighborhood spot where they could share their love for traditional Thai street food and culture as well as their commitment to best-quality, locally sourced ingredients.

Sen Yai Sen Lek (translation: Big Noodle Little Noodle), then, is truly a family venture. But for Hatch-Surisook, owning a restaurant is about so much more than owning a restaurant. "Food is the connection to personal and cultural experiences, celebrations, and gatherings with friends and family, a way into places—familiar or new—and the people in them. I enjoy our regulars who identify the food we prepare and serve as their comfort food. . . . Thai comfort food in Northeast Minneapolis, I think that's great. I enjoy being able to present Thai cuisine that has the stamp of approval of my mom and her Thai friends, that is prepared with care and integrity, that speaks to others' tastes and memories."

Needless to say, Sen Yai Sen Lek's loyal customers enjoy it, too, pairing locally brewed beer to fresh, vibrant appetizers like *po pia tod* (fresh Thai spring rolls with cucumber, marinated tofu, Chinese sausage, bean sprouts, egg, and green onion, served with tamarind sauce) and entrees like *laab gai* (spicy Isaan salad of chopped chicken with toasted rice powder, mint, lime and lemongrass) and namesake noodle dishes like *pad see lew gai* (stir-fried wide rice noodles with sweet soy, egg, marinated chicken, and Chinese broccoli).

A Boonmee Surisook drawing of the much-revered nineteenth-century King Rama V has watched over the happy guests since Sen Yai Sen Lek opened its doors in 2008 (as Hatch-Surisook points out, "just as the economy bottomed out!"). Given what a generous chef Hatch-Surisook is—a common refrain among other local chefs is, "I love Joe! Great guy, awesome cook!"—

we're all glad the Hatch-Surisooks rode the wave and and are still partnering with local farmers to bring traditional Thai food with a Minnesota twist to Northeast Minneapolis.

PAD BAI KAPRAO MOO

HOLY BASIL STIR-FRY WITH PORK

(SERVES 4)

2½ tablespoons fish sauce

2 tablespoons oyster sauce

2 teaspoons sugar

8 cloves garlic

5 Thai chiles, stemmed

2 tablespoons vegetable oil

1 pound coarse ground pork

½ cup sliced yellow onion

6 ounces long beans, cut into 1-inch pieces

2 cups loosely packed kaprao/Thai holy basil leaves (not to be confused with horapa/Thai basil, although if you cannot find kaprao, horapa is a suitable/tasty substitute)

For garnish:

4 crispy sunny-side up fried eggs

Steamed jasmine rice

Prik naam pla (fish sauce with Thai chiles)

In a small bowl, stir together the fish sauce, oyster sauce, and sugar. Set aside.

Crush garlic and Thai chiles together in a mortar and pestle (or roughly chop together). Heat a 12-inch skillet over medium-high heat. Add the oil and, when the oil is hot, stir-fry the garlic and chile mixture for about 15 seconds or until fragrant.

Increase heat to high and add the pork and onion. Stir-fry until pork is almost done, 2–3 minutes. Add the long beans and stir-fry for 1 minute.

Stir in sauce mixture and toss to coat the pork and long beans. Add basil leaves and toss until incorporated. Remove from heat.

Serve with steamed jasmine rice and top with a crispy fried egg and prik naam pla.

Neua Yang Nam Tok

Isaan Grilled Beef Salad

(SERVES 4)

Note: Begin preparing sticky rice several hours before you plan to serve the salad.

For the khao neow (steamed sticky rice):

2 cups raw sticky rice (sometimes called Thai sweet rice)

For the Isaan grilled beef salad:

4 tablespoons raw sticky rice
2 teaspoons plus 3½ tablespoons Thai fish sauce
1½ pounds flank steak or top sirloin
¼ cup freshly squeezed lime juice
2 tablespoons thinly sliced shallots
1–2 teaspoons Thai chile powder
2 tablespoons chopped green onions
2 tablespoons chopped cilantro
2 tablespoons chopped mint leaves
Khao neow (see above)

For garnish:

A variety of chopped raw vegetables, such as cucumbers, green beans, radishes, bitter greens, cabbage

To prepare sticky rice: Add rice to a large bowl and rinse the rice well under cold water three or four times. Cover the rice with cold water and allow it to soak for at least 6 hours; alternately, soak the rice in hot tap water for 3 hours.

Prepare a pot of boiling water fitted with a cheesecloth-lined steaming basket. Drain the rice and place it in the steaming basket, cover, and steam for 15–20 minutes. Remove rice from heat and transfer to a serving bowl. Cover rice and cool until just warm. As a reward for your efforts, pick up some of the rice with your hands, roll it into a ball, and pop it into your mouth. Enjoy! Keep rice warm for serving.

To make the salad: In a small, dry skillet over medium heat, toast raw sticky rice, shaking pan frequently, until rice turns a medium-brown color (being careful not to burn the rice). Remove from heat and cool completely. Grind rice into a powder using a coffee or spice grinder. Set aside 2 teaspoons of powder and store the rest in an airtight container for future use.

Rub 2 teaspoons of fish sauce on the flank steak and let sit at room temperature for about 30 minutes. In the meantime, preheat grill to very hot. Grill the flank steak about 3 minutes per side, so that the ends of the steak are medium-rare and the center of the steak is rare. (Be careful not to overcook the steak as the acid from the lime juice in the dressing will also continue to cook the steak, bringing the steak to medium-rare/medium.) Transfer steak from grill to a cutting board and let rest for approximately 5 minutes.

Slice the flank steak against the grain into thin slices. Transfer the sliced steak to a large mixing bowl and add remaining 3½ tablespoons fish sauce, lime juice, shallots, Thai chile powder, and green onions. Toss thoroughly, then add cilantro and mint, gently mixing until incorporated.

Serve salad with khao neow (sticky rice) and raw vegetables.

Solera Restaurant and Event Center

900 Hennepin Avenue South
Minneapolis, MN 55403
(612) 338-0062
SOLERA-RESTAURANT.COM
Owner: Lee Lynch
Executive Chef: Jorge Guzman

Solera opened big in 2003, bringing authentic Spanish tapas to Twin Citians who didn't yet realize they were crazy for tapas. It turned out that the sultry, salty flavors of Spain are the perfect antidote to Minnesota winters, and for several years, times were good. And then they weren't, until Solera changed hands in 2010 and Executive Chef Jorge Guzman took over the kitchen in 2011. The tapas are still an integral—and lovely—part of the menu, but Guzman fleshed out the entree listings as well, adding an emphasis on locally sourced, seasonal ingredients. After a life-changing 2013 trip to the Basque region of Spain, Guzman came back brimming with ideas and inspiration. He's channeled his special love for pork into hosting summer-evening pig roasts on Solera's roof. It's not surprising that pork, locally brewed beer, and the Minneapolis skyline make a pretty sweet combination.

Guzman has also founded an annual fund-raiser called Farm in the City, a farm dinner in reverse where local farmers come to Solera to chat with diners, and a whole bevy of local chefs volunteer to cook course after course with the bounty of the farmers' harvest, all to raise money for Youth Farm and Market Project, which provides free, year-round programming for young people. The event is a rollicking good time, with farmers, chefs, and

passionate eaters talking together about what everyone loves most: good food and doing good.

That all means that Guzman is a very busy chef, because Solera isn't just a popular spot for the pre- and post-theater crowd (the Orpheum Theater is next door); it's also a lively event center with a thousand-person capacity. But at its heart, Solera is still about the tapas. With a menu broken into Basque-inspired (that trip!), vegetable, fish and shellfish, and meats, there are tapas for every diner, with beautiful Spanish wines to drink alongside them. Go with a group, share everything, absolutely head up to the roof if it's warm outside, and have a beautiful evening with friends.

PORK TENDERLOIN WITH PIPERADE & CHICKPEA PUREE

(SERVES 8)

For the piperade:

2 tablespoons extra-virgin olive oil
1 cup small-dice Serrano ham
2 onions, julienned
3 red bell peppers, julienned
3 yellow bell peppers, julienned
6 garlic cloves, peeled and chopped
1 (45-ounce) can whole tomatoes, seeded and chopped
1 tablespoon paprika
3 tablespoons fresh thyme leaves
2 tablespoons sugar
1½ cups white wine
1½ cups chicken stock
Salt
Sherry vinegar

For the chickpea puree:

2 cups cooked or canned chickpeas, drained
1 tablespoon chopped preserved lemon
2 garlic cloves, peeled and chopped
Juice of 1 lemon
Vegetable stock
Salt

For the pork tenderloin:

¼ cup extra-virgin olive oil
10 garlic cloves, peeled and chopped
3 tablespoons coriander seeds, toasted and ground
3 tablespoons cumin seeds, toasted and ground
3 tablespoons dried oregano
2 tablespoons kosher salt
2 tablespoons tomato paste
½ bunch fresh cilantro, chopped
2 serrano peppers, chopped
2 ounces achiote paste

1½ cups orange juice
2 pork tenderloins

To make the piperade: Heat olive oil in a 12-inch skillet over medium heat. When oil is hot, add Serrano ham and cook until it is slightly crispy. Add onions and peppers to the pan and cook for 2–3 minutes. Stir in the garlic and cook for 1 minute, then add the tomatoes, paprika, thyme, sugar, and wine, and simmer to reduce by one-quarter. Add stock and simmer, uncovered, for 30 minutes, stirring occasionally. Season with salt and sherry vinegar to taste.

To make the chickpea puree: Combine chickpeas, preserved lemon, garlic, and lemon juice in the bowl of a blender. Blend, adding vegetable stock as needed to achieve a very smooth puree. Season with salt to taste.

To make pork tenderloin: Combine all ingredients but the pork in the bowl of a blender. Puree until smooth.

Put pork tenderloins in a 1-gallon sealable plastic bag. Pour in the marinade, press air from the bag, and seal. Refrigerate the pork, turning occasionally, for 12–24 hours.

Preheat grill on medium-high heat. Remove pork from marinade; discard marinade. Pat pork dry with paper towels. Grill pork, with the cover closed, for 7 minutes. Turn pork and grill for another 7 minutes, or until a thermometer inserted into the thickest portion registers 140°F. Wrap pork in aluminum foil and let rest for 10 minutes. Slice and serve with piperade and chickpea puree.

The Twin Cities craft beer scene has boomed in recent years, turning Minneapolis–St. Paul into a regional beer destination. Just a few short years ago, craft breweries in the Twin Cities were relatively sparse, until 2011 when, presto-chango, the "Surly law" was passed by the Minnesota legislature, and the whole landscape was transformed. Prior to passage, Minnesota law barred production breweries from selling pints on-site. Without the vital source of revenue that taprooms provide, the old law squelched the growth of new breweries and prevented a craft-brew movement from taking hold. With the law change, pent-up demand for craft brews has been unleashed, and new breweries are popping up every few months. Needless to say, craft beer lovers are in hoppy heaven. While most taprooms don't prepare food, a beautiful collaboration with our vibrant food truck scene has quickly evolved, ensuring taproom patrons beer-friendly eats to wash down with craft IPAs.

The proliferation of breweries has fueled an exploration of expanding beer styles and flavorings. Many Minnesota craft beers rely on unique ingredients such as local honey, unique hop varieties, and ingredients like sweet yams and fiery habanero peppers. Coffee, fruits, and local herbs are not unusual enhancements, opening the

door to a whole new level of food-and-beer pairing dinners and restaurant specials; as you can imagine, local chefs are thrilled be offering an ever-expanding selection of locally sourced brews.

Perhaps the best part of the taproom scene is sampling a fresh pint—often from revolving taps—brewed just a stone's throw away while visiting with passionate and knowledgeable staff. As a bonus, you can carry away a growler (a half gallon) of freshly tapped beer to drink at home. Such intimate access is changing the way Twin Citians think about and drink beer, aided by our local food media who have jumped on updating taproom guides and putting together maps and reviews of both beers and taproom experiences. Taproom crawls and even bus tours have popped up to meet the demand of beer-crazy Minnesotans. With seventeen taprooms and counting, there's a beer for everyone, in all parts of the metro, no matter your preference. See the Minnesota Craft Brewers Guild website at mncraftbrew.org for a comprehensive list of breweries as well as news and events.

FULTON BREWING COMPANY

BRIAN HOFFMAN, CO-OWNER

GAME-DAY ARTICHOKE DIP

(SERVES 4)

Note: There is no doubt that this dip is delicious with Fulton Lonely Blonde.

2 cans quartered artichoke hearts, drained well, each
    quarter cut into 3 pieces
2 cups shredded Monterey Jack cheese
1 cup shredded Parmesan cheese
2 cloves garlic, peeled and minced or crushed
2 teaspoons freshly squeezed lemon juice
½ cup mayonnaise, or more as needed
Salt and freshly ground black pepper

For serving:

Crusty bread
Assorted crackers

Preheat oven to 350°F. In a large bowl, stir together artichoke hearts, cheeses, garlic, and lemon juice. Fold in mayonnaise—the goal is to just bind the ingredients; only add a bit more if needed to evenly incorporate the artichoke hearts and cheese. Season with salt to taste and with several grinds of black pepper.

Spread mixture in a pie plate or other shallow, oven-safe baking dish. Bake 20–30 minutes or until melted, bubbly, and the top is turning golden brown and delicious. Serve hot with crusty bread and/or crackers.

Sonora Grill

920 E. Lake Street
Minneapolis, MN 55407
(612) 871-1900
sonora-grill.com
Co-Owners: Alejandro Castillon and Conrado Paredes
Executive Chef: Alejandro Castillon

It's a terrific story: Immigrants Conrado Paredes and Alejandro Castillon, long-time friends from the Mexican state of Sonora, after years of cooking around the Twin Cities, decide to open a taco stand at Midtown Global Market in Minneapolis. After cultivating what can only be described as a slightly maniacal fan base (read: people lining up at the door), Paredes and Castillon have expanded their spicy reach with a just-opened, sit-down restaurant a few miles down Lake Street.

What's their magic formula? It doesn't hurt that the two are gracious as well as movie-star handsome, but the key to Sonora Grill's success is solid, boldly flavored, everything-from-scratch cooking. After ten years spent in some of the top kitchens in town, Executive Chef Castillon crafted a Latin-fusion menu, marrying favorite Spanish, Mexican, and South American ingredients with an emphasis on delicious. While the Midtown Global Market stand will stick to fast-casual favorites like warm tortillas filled with tender pork *guajillo* and fresh chiles, *bocadillo* sandwiches stuffed with crispy eggplant, house-made hot dogs bathed in chimichurri, and some of the best hand-cut fries in town, the new location offers Castillon even more room to flex his culinary muscles. With a spacious kitchen, table-side service, and a full bar headed up by bartender Raul Saud, Sonora's offerings have expanded to include appetizers, plated entrees, and fresh, snappy cocktails, which now makes Sonora Grill a top contender for the best spot in town to both acquire (with tequila) and cure (with tacos) a hangover. Excelente!

Mariscada

(SERVES 4–6)

Note: Serve mariscada with warm corn tortillas and a very simple salad of lettuce, tomatoes, and red onion dressed with lime juice, olive oil, and salt. And a good, cold Mexican beer!

6 teaspoons olive oil, divided
1 large russet potato, peeled and quartered
2 stalks celery, cut into 2-inch pieces
1 large yellow onion, peeled and quartered
4 red bell peppers, cut into 2-inch pieces
2 New Mexico peppers, coarsely chopped
1 clove garlic, halved
3 teaspoons salt
1 teaspoon black pepper
1 teaspoon ground coriander
1 teaspoon ground cumin
½ teaspoon dried oregano
3 cups Clamato
1 gallon vegetable stock
½ pound barramundi or sea bass, cut into 2-inch pieces
½ pound clams, scrubbed
½ pound mussels, scrubbed
½ pound sea scallops

Add 3 teaspoons olive oil to a dutch oven or other large pot set over medium-high heat. When oil is hot, add vegetables and garlic and sauté, stirring occasionally, for 10 minutes. Add salt, pepper, spices, and Clamato and simmer for 5 minutes. Add vegetable stock and simmer, uncovered, until potato is very soft and vegetables are tender, 20 minutes.

Working in batches, puree sauce in a blender until smooth. Season to taste with salt. Reserve.

Add 3 teaspoons olive oil to a 12-inch skillet set over medium-high heat. When oil is hot, add fish and shellfish and cook for 3–4 minutes. Turn fish and add 4 cups sauce to the pan. Bring to a simmer and cook until fish is just done and shellfish are opened (discard unopened shells), about 4 minutes. Serve hot in bowls. (Cover and refrigerate any leftover sauce.)

The Hermosillo Cocktail

(MAKES 1 COCKTAIL)

1¼ ounces tequila (Familia Camarena Tequila preferred)

¼ ounce mezcal (Auténtico Mezcal Alacrán preferred)

¾ ounce orange juice

1 ounce lime juice

¾ ounce simple syrup

3 dried hibiscus flowers

Strips of lemon zest, for garnish

Combine ingredients (except lemon zest) in a large shaker or glass filled with ice. Cover and shake well. Pour into a rocks glass filled with fresh ice. Garnish with lemon zest twist.

THE STRIP CLUB MEAT & FISH

378 MARIA AVENUE
ST. PAUL, MN 55106
(651) 793-6247
DOMEATS.COM
CO-OWNER: TIM NIVER
EXECUTIVE CHEF/CO-OWNER: JD FRATZKE

It always feels a bit naughty to say you're heading to The Strip Club for dinner, which is just how co-owners Tim Niver and Executive Chef JD Fratzke like it. The Strip Club is a meaty, masculine place, dark and sexy with world-class hospitality, not to mention luscious cocktails. When you walk in the door, prepare to be warmly welcomed by Niver to the best dinner party in St. Paul.

As you read over the menu, you'll notice that Executive Chef Fratzke loves words as much as he loves grass-fed beef. With standards like Meat to Please You and Sin-Sin-Naughty-Poutine, Fratzke swirls together best-quality, farm-fresh ingredients, sassy literature references, and a whole lotta love to crank out plate after plate of some of the most award-winning food in either of our fair cities. And I mean plate after plate—it is always packed at The Strip Club, for dinner as well as brunch on the weekends.

The restaurant sits charmingly atop Dayton's Bluff, one of St. Paul's oldest neighborhoods. The circa-1885 building reminds you that St. Paul has a saucy history,

while those sparkling cocktails remind you that it had something to do with Prohibition. Thank goodness those days are past because the craft cocktails at The Strip Club are much tastier than bathtub gin. Much. Tastier. Pull up a stool and order off the menu or describe your favorite elements—try (post-Prohibition) gin, thyme, and bubbles, for instance, like I have on any number of occasions—and let the bartenders work their magic with house-made bitters, mixers, and garnishes, as well as fresh juices and herbs. Soon you'll be chatting with your barmates, and Niver, and Fratzke when he checks in with his diners, and the bartenders when you have them make up another drink for you. . . . and you'll see exactly why The Strip Club is so beloved.

The team recently announced plans for a new downtown St. Paul eatery, opening in 2014. Called Saint Dinette, the concept is hospitality-focused, of course, but this time with a European twist, straight up. St. Paul eagerly awaits its newest saint.

GINBALL WIZARD COCKTAIL

(SERVES 1)

2 ounces gin (Beefeater preferred)
¼ ounce yellow Chartreuse
¼ ounce Benedictine
4 drops cherry vanilla bitters

For garnish:

Lemon twist
Brandied cherry

Fill a rocks glass with ice. In a shaker or large glass, combine gin, Chartreuse, Benedictine, and bitters. Pour over ice and garnish with a lemon twist and a brandied cherry. Enjoy!

Duck Tataki

(SERVES 8)

For the ginger-lemongrass vinaigrette (makes about 2 cups):

5 ounces fresh ginger, peeled and grated
4 ounces pulverized lemongrass pulp
5 limes, zested and juiced
¼ cup rice vinegar
1 tablespoon roasted garlic puree
1 teaspoon sea salt
½ teaspoon cayenne pepper
½ cup Minnesota honey
1½ cups blended oil (a combination of canola and olive oil works well)

For the miso-chestnut sauce (makes about 3 cups):

2 cups chicken stock
½ cup mirin
1 tablespoon Thai fish sauce
2 tablespoons thinly sliced, peeled fresh ginger
2 tablespoons miso paste
2 cups roasted, peeled chestnuts
2 teaspoons granulated sugar
Sea salt

For the duck:

4 (6- to 8-ounce) boneless duck breasts, fat cap scored, seasoned generously with salt and black pepper
2 tablespoons canola oil
1 cup miso-chestnut sauce (see recipe)
1 Anjou or Asian pear, halved, cored, grilled, sliced ⅛-inch thick
Juice of ½ lime
½ ounce fresh ginger, peeled and sliced as thinly as possible
4 ounces salad mix (a combination of celery leaves, fresh parsley, chopped basil, frisée; or a simple mesclun mix)

2 tablespoons ginger-lemongrass vinaigrette (see recipe)

To make the vinaigrette: Combine ginger, lemongrass pulp, lime juice and zest, vinegar, garlic, salt, cayenne, and honey, in a blender and puree on highest setting for 30 seconds. Reduce speed to lowest setting and drizzle in blended oil until emulsified. Cover and chill until ready to use.

To make the sauce: Place all ingredients except sugar and salt in a large saucepan and set over medium heat. When mixture bubbles, turn heat to low and simmer, uncovered, for 20 minutes.

Remove sauce from heat and stir in sugar. Working in batches, puree chestnut mixture in a blender, starting at lowest speed and slowly progressing to highest speed. Be aware that blending hot liquids requires extra care, so never overfill the container. Pass the sauce through a fine mesh strainer and season to taste with sea salt. Cool to room temperature, then cover and refrigerate until ready to use.

To prepare the duck: Pat the duck breasts dry with a paper towel.

Heat canola oil in a 12-inch sauté pan over medium heat. When oil is hot and shimmering, use tongs to lay 2 breasts skin side down into the pan.

Sauté the breasts without turning for 4–5 minutes or until skin becomes crisp and toffee brown. Using the tongs, very carefully flip the duck breasts to sear the flesh side for 30 seconds only. Transfer breasts, skin side up, to a large plate and set aside to rest.

Repeat the process with remaining 2 duck breasts. (Reserve the hot oil, cool, strain into a jar, cover, and store in the refrigerator to use for sautéing vegetables, fish, or eggs, like your grandmother did with bacon fat).

When duck breasts have cooled enough to handle with your bare fingers, transfer the uncovered plate to the refrigerator and chill breasts for a minimum of 3 hours.

To serve: Slice duck breasts ¼ inch thick. Spoon miso-chestnut sauce onto a serving platter. Lay alternating slices of duck breast and sliced

pear onto the platter. Squeeze fresh lime juice over the pear and duck, then evenly scatter with ginger. Toss salad mix in a small bowl with ginger-lemongrass vinaigrette and season with salt and pepper. Evenly distribute the salad over the duck and pear.

Generously pour yourself something light and chilled and toast your guests, internally celebrating your new command of wild game and the good life in the great state of Minnesota. I say internally because we're Minnesotans. We're modest. It's the law.

The Strip Club
Meat & Fish

Drink List
$10

The Libertine
Laird's Applejack, St. Elizabeth Allspice Dram, house-made sour, Easy & Oskey Black Walnut Bitters

Broad Strokes
Bourbon, Campari, Farigoule, Peychaud's Bitters

Pretty in Drink (Kegged/On Tap)
Vodka, Galliano, lemonade, grapefruit juice, honey syrup, Easy & Oskey Apricot Bitters

Spanish Fly (Kegged/On Tap)
Wine, Brandy, OJ, Rose Cognac, Cava

Cobra Kai
Kilo Kai Rum, Easy & Oskey Habanero Bi...
house-made sour

Wine List

Red

	Glass/Bottle
Vinchio–Vaglio Serra, Barbera, Italy	
Filon, Garnacha, Spain	$6/24
Padrillos, Malbec, Argentina	$7/28
Pozzan, Annabella, Cabernet Sauvignon, CA	$9/36
Vietti, Nebbiolo, Piemonte, Italy	$12/48
Chinon, Cabernet Franc, France	$42
Jacuzzi Family Vineyards, Barb...	$45

SUN STREET BREADS

4600 NICOLLET AVENUE
MINNEAPOLIS, MN 55419
(612) 354-3414
SUNSTREETBREADS.COM
OWNER AND HEAD BAKER: SOLVEIG TOFTE

Thank goodness for procrastination, because that's how the Twin Cities acquired one of the best bakers in the country. When Solveig Tofte took baking breaks from college cramming, she discovered her life's passion. "I figured out I wasn't meant for sitting in meetings all day. I had always wanted a trade, a practical skill that would be useful wherever I went. So I chose baking and haven't looked back."

Tofte made a name for herself locally as the long-time head baker at the award-winning Turtle Bread Company in Minneapolis, and nationally as the captain and breads representative on the Bread Bakers Guild Team USA 2008 at the Coupe du Monde de la Boulangerie in Paris. In 2009, she was named to the Board of the Bread Bakers Guild of America.

Tofte and her husband, Martin Ouimet, initially launched Sun Street Breads as a farmers' market stand in 2009, and to say it was a smash hit is a bit of an understatement. While Tofte and her baking crew sold breads and pastries as fast as they could bake them, Ouimet perfected recipes like Sun Street's top-notch french fries (in my opinion, the best in the Twin Cities) and nailed down plans for the brick-and-mortar restaurant they opened to acclaim in 2010.

Sun Street Breads is a sunny, cheerful addition to Minneapolis's Kingfield neighborhood. While bread lovers are naturally drawn to the baskets of golden, crusty loaves—not to mention piles of buttery cookies, tarts, and biscuits—those of us who adore artisan tilework ooh and aah over Sun Street's smiling logo set into the bakery's main wall. The signature blue tiles were handmade and mounted by Kirsten Walstead of SoMi Tileworks. Tofte notes on behalf of her friend Walstead, "Be sure to check out the basket-weave tiles in the bathrooms!"

Fast casual is the name of the dining game in the Twin Cities these days, and Sun Street is part of the trend. Open for breakfast and lunch only—except for pizza night on

Sun Street Breads 169

CRUSHER COOKIE
Chocolate chip with crushed
sugar cones and pretzels

$1.75

Monday—diners place orders at the counter for breakfast classics like sausage and biscuits or for high-end sandwiches alongside those killer fries. Sun Street's relaxed, family-friendly atmosphere reflects Tofte's and Ouimet's roles as parents who also live in the neighborhood.

In fact, Tofte developed the Crusher Cookies recipe with her young daughter, Linnea, who decided a sugar cone cookie would be delicious. They worked on several iterations to find the perfect balance of sweet and salty, then named the cookies after the United Crushers silo near Tofte's childhood home in southeast Minneapolis. "I love silos and graffiti, and my cousin says the United Crushers graffiti crew wouldn't mind having a cookie named after their work."

CRUSHER COOKIES

(MAKES 24 LARGE COOKIES)

1 cup (2 sticks) unsalted butter, room temperature

¾ cup granulated sugar

½ cup brown sugar

1 tablespoon honey

2 teaspoons vanilla extract

2 large eggs

1½ cups all-purpose flour

½ teaspoon baking soda

1½ teaspoons baking powder

1 teaspoon salt

18 small pretzels (about 1 ounce), crushed into 1-inch pieces

12 sugar cones, crushed into 1-inch pieces

½ cup bittersweet chocolate chips

Preheat oven to 350°F. Line two baking sheets with parchment paper.

In the bowl of a stand mixer fitted with the paddle attachment, cream together butter, sugars, honey, and vanilla until smooth.

Add the eggs and mix until lumpy. Using a rubber spatula, scrape down the bowl, then continue beating at medium speed until mixture is smooth.

In a separate large bowl, stir together the flour, baking soda, baking powder, and salt. Add to the butter mixture and mix on low speed until just combined, scraping down the bowl once or twice to make sure flour is evenly incorporated.

Add pretzel and sugar cone pieces and mix on low speed until just combined. Stir in chocolate chips.

Using a medium ice-cream scoop, place dough on lined baking sheets, leaving 2 inches between cookies. Flatten each scoop of dough slightly, then bake for 12 minutes or until evenly browned. Cool on racks; store in airtight container.

TILIA

2726 W. 43RD STREET
MINNEAPOLIS, MN 55410
(612) 354-2806
TILIAMPLS.COM
CO-OWNER: JORG PIERACH
CO-OWNER/EXECUTIVE CHEF: STEVEN BROWN

The first time I enjoyed Executive Chef Steven Brown's food was in 2003, back when he was running the kitchen at a restaurant called RockStar. Our friend Andrew Zimmern told us to eat there, with the advice that Brown's cooking was the best thing going in Minneapolis. I ordered braised short ribs, and they were so perfectly rich, tender, and beefy, I went back the next night and had the same dish all over again. I still think about those ribs.

It turns out that humble food made sublime is Brown's specialty. With a long and highly respected career in the Twin Cities—many successful local chefs tip their hats to Brown for inspiring them to cook and for making them better at what they do—Brown can finesse any ingredient thrown at him. But he's made the decision, with Tilia, to keep

the menu Midwestern and approachable, in a cozy-chic space where he himself would like to spend time and eat with his family and friends.

Tilia is all that and more. From its name—*tilia* is Latin for "linden," a reference to the picturesque Linden Hills neighborhood that the restaurant calls home—to its design, menu, and vibe, Tilia is a neighborhood hang in every sense, that rare restaurant that has achieved a symbiotic relationship with its neighbors. Open pretty much all day, every day (closed briefly between brunch and dinner on the weekends), it's fair to say that Tilia is always bustling. The crowd changes with the time of day, in varying combinations of business meetings, moms and kids, ladies who lunch, couples out for date night, groups of jovial friends, and late-night revelers. The menu shifts, too, from lunch to "in-between" to dinner to late night. It's not easy to fill a restaurant as consistently as Tilia does it, but by really knowing his customers and delivering exactly what they love with top-notch customer service, Brown has created a true Minneapolis gem.

While Tilia's food is approachable, Brown hasn't been a multiple James Beard Award Semifinalist for Best Chef Midwest, and Tilia didn't win the 2012 Charlie Award for Outstanding Restaurant (plus many other local media awards for best restaurant) without delivering stunning, unique dishes that send diners over the moon. Grilled chicken thighs are served with chorizo, pickled pineapple, and black bean–Oaxaca cheese fondue. A BLT is tarted up with chicken liver pâté, romaine, bacon, and cherry tomatoes on a buttermilk bun. Rainbow trout is made memorable with *sinigang*, bone marrow, and Chinese green beans. You get the picture. And it is divine.

While Brown is clearly having a blast taking his turn as restaurateur, like for many chefs, it comes down to the diners. "I am fascinated with what a friend once described as 'the sociology of food, restaurants, and people,' but if I had to say only one word, I'd say *people*. Without people, I'd be cooking dinner for myself, by myself every night. Not nearly as much fun!"

KNÖDEL

(MAKES 25–30 DUMPLINGS)

Chef Brown's note: This is a winter recipe if there ever was one. You can cook the dumplings in advance and sauté them in a little butter to reheat.

16 ounces dried bread, diced

1 cup milk

1 yellow onion, finely chopped

3 tablespoons unsalted butter

1½ tablespoons olive oil

3 large eggs, lightly beaten

3 tablespoons finely chopped flat-leaf parsley

8 ounces Parmesan cheese, grated

½ cup all-purpose flour, plus more for dusting knödel

¾ teaspoon kosher salt, plus more for the cooking water

½ teaspoon freshly ground black pepper

¼ teaspoon freshly ground nutmeg

3–4 quarts water for cooking knödel

For the garnishes:

Brown butter

Freshly squeezed lemon juice

Pea puree

Crème fraîche

Place bread in large mixing bowl. In a small saucepan over medium-low heat, heat the milk until it is hot and pour it over the bread. Let stand for 15 minutes.

In a 10-inch skillet over medium heat, sauté the onion in butter and oil until translucent, about 10 minutes. Add to bread mixture. Add the remaining ingredients (except the cooking water) and knead into a soft doughlike mass.

Bring water to a boil and season with enough salt to taste but not overpower it.

Form a knödel into a ball about the size of a golf ball and lightly dust with flour on the outside so it is not sticky. Drop into boiling water as a test. If it falls apart, add a bit more flour to dough (not too much). Once satisfied with the texture, roll the remaining dough into balls and dust with flour. Cook in boiling water for 10–15 minutes (they will expand as they cook).

Drain and serve with brown butter, lemon juice, pea puree, and crème fraîche.

Victory 44

2203 N. 44th Avenue
Minneapolis, MN 55412
(612) 588-2228
victory-44.com
Owner/Executive Chef: Erick Harcey

If dog owners and dogs resemble each other, perhaps the same could be true for chefs and their restaurants. Think about that, then consider Erick Harcey and his flagship gastropub, Victory 44 in north Minneapolis. Rustic-meets-refined is the theme that traces through Harcey's personal story as well as through Victory 44's decor and menu.

Raised in a small town north of the Twin Cities, Harcey landed in Minneapolis for culinary school and worked initially with pastry and fine chocolates. As he branched out into running restaurants, and then into opening Victory 44 in 2009, Harcey made a name for himself working both ends of the culinary spectrum: butchery craftsman meets molecular gastronomer. Clearly enjoying wearing many hats, Harcey jumps around from chef, prankster, hunter, husband, father of four, and businessman with ease and good humor.

Like Harcey, Victory 44 itself comfortably straddles the line between casual and polished. Reclaimed wood tables—finished by Harcey's father after Harcey bought the wood on a whim—are knotty, glossy showstoppers in an otherwise light and simple space. Menus

are written on chalkboards, and chefs themselves bring food to the tables. As both a coffee shop and restaurant, Victory 44 functions as a neighborhood joint and Friday-night-out destination.

From my perspective, the plates Harcey delivers from the kitchen are a food photographer's delight. Items that read as deceptively simple on the menu—roasted chicken or beet salad—arrive beautifully composed, layered with texture and color. Despite the level of craft, this isn't fancy food. The coffee bar serves locally roasted Dogwood coffee, scratch-baked treats, and hearty breakfasts. The restaurant is as casual or spiffy as you want it to be, full of neighborhood regulars drinking locally brewed beer and eating Perfect Burgers, or sparkly ladies sipping bubbles and swooning over Harcey's beautiful salads and roasted vegetables (with a side of bacon fries "to share").

Like so many chefs, what Harcey enjoys most is having an impact on the people enjoying the food he creates. "I obviously love working with the products and finding new techniques, but I also love watching someone just really experience a flavor or texture for the first time and not even be able to process their feelings. I honestly just love every bit about being a chef!"

CHICKEN LIVER MOUSSE WITH PICKLED BLUEBERRIES

(MAKES SIX 4-OUNCE SERVINGS)

For the pickled blueberries (makes 4 cups):

1 cup apple cider vinegar
½ cup sugar
1¾ tablespoons salt
2 thyme sprigs
1 quart (4 cups) fresh blueberries
2 shallots, peeled and sliced

For the mousse:

Splash of olive oil
4 minced shallots
4 strips of bacon, julienned
3 minced garlic cloves
2 thyme sprigs
1 pound cleaned chicken livers
¼ cup bourbon
¾ pound unsalted butter (3 sticks)
¾ cup heavy cream
Sea salt
Freshly ground black pepper
6 tablespoons unsalted butter (¾ stick), melted

For serving:

Pickled blueberries (see recipe)
Crackers

To make the pickled blueberries: Combine vinegar, sugar, salt, and thyme sprigs in a large saucepan. Set pan over medium-high heat and bring brine to a boil. Remove pan from heat and let cool for 4 minutes.

Stir in blueberries and shallots, then set aside to cool completely before serving. (Cover and chill any leftover blueberries.)

To prepare the mousse: Add olive oil to a heavy-bottomed, 12-inch skillet set over medium heat. When oil is hot, add shallots, bacon, garlic, and thyme and sauté, stirring frequently, until caramelized, about 15 minutes.

Add chicken livers and sauté, stirring a few times, until livers are cooked halfway through, about 5 minutes. Carefully add bourbon (noting that it's flammable) and cook until au sec (almost dry), about 5 minutes.

Transfer mixture to the bowl of a blender, discarding thyme sprigs. With the blender on low speed, slowly add butter, and then cream. Season to taste with salt and pepper. Press mixture through a chinois, then transfer to 4-ounce jars or ramekins. Cool to room temperature, then top each with ¼ inch of melted butter. Cover and chill until cold.

Serve with crackers and pickled blueberries. Can be refrigerated for up to one week.

DEVILS ON HORSEBACK

(MAKES 30)

Note: Blue whiz requires an iSi cream charger. Alternatively, you could serve it as a warm cheese sauce.

For the date puree (makes about 1 cup):

1 cup pitted dates
1 (12-ounce) bottle ginger beer
Zest and juice of 1 lemon
1 tablespoon chopped, peeled fresh ginger
2 star anise pods
2 tablespoons sherry vinegar
1 tablespoon unsalted butter

For the blue whiz (makes 2 cups):

1 cup whole milk
4 ounces Velveeta cheese, cubed
4 ounces smoked blue cheese, crumbled
3 drops hot sauce

For the devils:

30 pitted dates
1 pound blue cheese (preferably smoked)
15 strips par-cooked bacon, halved crosswise
30 toothpicks or short skewers

For the garnish (optional):

Chopped chives
Chopped toasted almonds

To make the date puree: Combine all ingredients in a large saucepan. Set over medium heat and bring to a boil. Turn heat to low and simmer, uncovered, for 20 minutes.

Transfer mixture to the bowl of a blender and puree until smooth. Cool to room temperature.

To make the blue whiz: Combine ingredients in a large saucepan set over medium heat. Stir until cheeses are melted. Pass cheese sauce through chinois.

Pour sauce into iSi charger and charge twice, shaking hard between each charge. Chill in refrigerator for 1 hour. Shake hard once again before serving.

To make the devils: Stuff each date with blue cheese, then wrap in bacon. Skewer each with a toothpick to secure bacon.

In a 12-inch skillet over medium heat, fry the devils in batches, turning a few times, until bacon is crispy on all sides, transferring devils to a baking sheet as you go.

To serve: Preheat oven to 400°F. Bake devils for 7–8 minutes or until hot. Serve with date puree and blue whiz, garnished with chopped chives and chopped almonds.

Persimmon & Pea Tendril Salad with Whipped Burrata & Ginger Vinaigrette

(SERVES 4)

Note: This recipe requires an iSi cream charger to make the whipped burrata. Alternatively, you could serve whole burrata instead.

For the ginger vinaigrette (makes ½ cup):

3 tablespoons rice vinegar
1 tablespoon freshly grated ginger
1 teaspoon minced shallots
1 tablespoon honey
¼ cup vegetable oil
Sea salt
Freshly ground black pepper

For the salad:

4 ounces burrata, room temperature
6 ounces heavy cream
Sea salt
1 cup fresh peas (from 1 pound pea pods)
1 cup pea tendrils
2 teaspoons toasted sesame seeds
1 tablespoon chopped chives
4 ripe persimmons, cut into bite-size wedges
Freshly ground black pepper

To make the vinaigrette: Whisk vinegar, ginger, shallots, honey, and oil together in a small bowl. Season to taste with salt and pepper. (Cover and refrigerate any unused vinaigrette.)

To make the salad: Place burrata in the bowl of a blender. Warm cream, then pour over burrata. Puree burrata and cream in blender until very smooth (no lumps). Season with salt to taste. Cool mixture to room temperature, then transfer to an iSi charger, charge two times, and chill in the refrigerator.

Set out a large bowl of ice water. Fill a large saucepan with salted water and bring to a boil over high heat. Blanch peas in boiling water for 1 minute, drain, and quickly add peas to ice bath (to halt cooking). Chill peas in ice bath for 3–4 minutes, then drain in a colander.

In a medium bowl, combine peas, pea tendrils, toasted sesame seeds, and chopped chives. Toss with enough ginger vinaigrette to coat lightly.

To serve: Divide salad among four plates. Arrange persimmon slices on the plates. (Shake iSi canister very well and shoot a trial spray of burrata onto a separate dish.) Squirt dollops of whipped burrata alongside the salad. Season with salt and freshly ground black pepper and serve.

VINCENT A RESTAURANT

1100 NICOLLET AVENUE
MINNEAPOLIS, MN 55403
(612) 630-1189
VINCENTARESTAURANT.COM
OWNER AND EXECUTIVE CHEF: VINCENT FRANCOUAL

Read this with a French accent, and you'll have a sense of how Executive Chef Vincent Francoual brightened the corner of Nicollet and 11th in downtown Minneapolis when he opened Vincent A Restaurant in 2001. Born in Puy-L'Eveque, in the Cahors region of France, Francoual began his culinary training at age fifteen. "At first it was the opportunity to get a quick job and travel along the world. Then I really got passionate with the 'craft of food.' I found it is spiritual, magic to transform food into recipes."

After years of cooking in France, Francoual arrived in the Twin Cities by way of New York. After honing his skills in the kitchens of Le Bernadin and Lespinasse, his then-wife was transferred to Minnesota in 1997, et voilà, Minneapolis was serendipitously gifted with one of its most cherished chefs. Francoual took over the kitchen at Cafe Un Deux Trois and earned a fast following of diners eager for his fresh take on French classics. While he put plans in motion to open his own restaurant, he catered and taught cooking classes to culinary students and home cooks, building a network of chefs and customers who are friends to this day.

Despite the steady success of Vincent A Restaurant over the last thirteen years, and being named a 2010 James Beard Award Semifinalist for Best Chef Midwest, Francoual isn't content to rest on his laurels. "As a chef, I am still searching for my style. I love cooking the traditional French dishes, but I am also curious about exploring the culinary world."

While most of Francoual's creative time is spent training new chefs, updating classic French presentations, overseeing a top-notch wine program, and pleasing crowds with dishes like the award-winning braised-short-rib-stuffed Vincent Burger, Francoual is still a popular cooking class instructor and go-to TV demo chef. He was the winner of the 2010 *Minnesota Monthly* Local Chef Challenge cooking competition—a $10,000 award that he spent, but of course, on a trip to France to compete in the Coeur d'Alene Ironman Competition.

How does Francoual balance a busy life as restaurant owner, chef, instructor, athlete, and new father? "Every morning when I start the day in the kitchen, it is my ambition to create beauty and happiness. I feel fortunate that I can make my living doing this."

PRAWNS WITH WHITE BEANS, AVOCADO & ORANGE

(SERVES 4)

Note: Beans need to be started a day before serving.

8 ounces dried tarbais or other white beans, soaked overnight in water to cover, drained

1 bay leaf

1 whole clove

1 peeled garlic clove

½ small onion, peeled

¼ cup heavy cream

Kosher salt

1 ripe avocado, peeled and cut into ¼-inch dice

1 orange, peeled, segmented, and cut into ¼-inch dice

2 tablespoons extra-virgin olive oil, divided

Juice of 1 lemon

6 tablespoons Armagnac or cognac

1 tablespoon unsalted butter

12 prawns, heads intact, bodies shelled and deveined (Vincent uses New Caledonia blue prawns, but any size 13–14 will work)

Place soaked, drained beans in a dutch oven. Cover beans with water by 2 inches, add bay leaf, clove, garlic, and onion and set over medium-high heat. Bring to a boil, cover, then turn heat to low and simmer beans until tender, 1–1½ hours. Reserve ½ cup cooking liquid, then drain beans in a colander and return beans to dutch oven.

Transfer roughly a quarter of the beans to a blender. In a small saucepan over medium heat, bring cream to a boil. Add hot cream to the beans in the blender and puree until very smooth. Stir puree into beans in dutch oven and season to taste with salt. Keep warm.

In a small bowl, stir together the avocado and orange with 1 tablespoon olive oil and 1 tablespoon lemon juice. Season to taste with salt and set aside.

Add Armagnac to a small glass bowl and microwave for 10–15 seconds or until warm. Set nearby.

Heat remaining olive oil and butter in a 12-inch skillet over high heat. When oil is hot, add prawns and cook for 3 minutes. Turn prawns and cook for 2 minutes, then add warm Armagnac and pull the pan from heat. Light a long match or lighter, stand back from the pan, and light (flambé) the surface of the Armagnac to burn off the alcohol.

To serve, set out four plates. Spoon warm beans onto the center of the plate. Remove heads from shrimp and squeeze shrimp-head juice on top of beans. Divide shrimp among plates, settling on top of the beans. Spoon any pan juices over the shrimp. Spoon avocado-orange salad alongside shrimp and beans.

WISE ACRE EATERY

5401 NICOLLET AVENUE SOUTH
MINNEAPOLIS, MN 55419
(612) 354-2577
WISEACREEATERY.COM
CO-OWNERS: SCOTT ENDRES AND DEAN ENGELMANN
EXECUTIVE CHEF: BETH FISHER

Wise Acre Eatery isn't a restaurant on a farm, but it's awfully close. In 2002, Scott Endres and Dean Engelmann founded Tangletown Gardens and Farm, to provide landscape and gardening design and sustainably raised plants to the residents of south Minneapolis. With the dreamy, fairyland garden center located in the city, sourced by the hundred-acre farm located in Plato, Minnesota, Endres and Engelmann spent several years beautifying yards all over town before they made a solid leap into food. After first adding a weekly farmers' market to the Tangletown Gardens location, a community sponsored agriculture (CSA) program that quickly grew to four hundred shares, and then hosting farm dinners in Plato, they were ready to go all-in when the business across the street from the garden center went up for sale in 2011. . . . and Wise Acre Eatery was born.

Executive Chef Beth Fisher was a natural choice to head the restaurant. A farm-to-table alum of Lucia's Restaurant in Minneapolis, Fisher was more than comfortable cooking seasonally with and planning menus around daily deliveries from local farms. The trick—and the luxury—with Wise Acre has been to plan ahead for ingredients with a deeper understanding of growing season and quantity. From Scottish Highland cattle, Berkshire Hogs, chickens and fresh eggs, and of course the gorgeous bounty of produce, Fisher's menu is as farm driven as it gets. "I love the pure creativity of having super-fresh ingredients for my dishes."

The charm of Tangletown Gardens has trailed right on across the street to Wise Acre Eatery. Luscious plantings adorn the popular patio and the tables inside, too, giving the casual neighborhood setting—Wise Acre, like the garden center, is beloved by its Tangletown neighbors—a feel as fresh as the food. The cozy, everything-from-scratch menu appeals to all ages and palates, from brunch classics like CSA hash topped with farm-fresh eggs and Berkshire bacon, to a juicy Highland beef burger with hand-cut fries and sparkling house-made sodas.

Fisher spent her childhood making big family meals with her Southern grandmother, and it shows: Wise Acre is at once welcoming, elegant, and always, always hopping. As Fisher says, "Food and entertaining are in my blood—bringing people together around a table to enjoy each other and a meal is very rewarding. The simplicity of good, farm-fresh ingredients makes my food sing. My presentation on the plate makes our customers sing. What's not to love?"

DILL PICKLE FRIED CHICKEN

(SERVES 6; RECIPE EASILY DOUBLED)

6 bone-in chicken thighs

6 chicken legs

4 cups dill pickle brine (from your favorite dill pickles)

4 cups all-purpose flour

¼ cup salt

3 tablespoons black pepper

1 quart buttermilk

6 cups vegetable oil for frying (peanut, safflower, sunflower, or other oil labeled for high-heat frying)

1 cup roughly chopped dill pickles

1 tablespoon chopped fresh dill

Place chicken thighs and legs in a large bowl and add pickle brine. Chicken pieces should be completely submerged in brine; use a small plate to weigh down the chicken if necessary. Cover bowl with plastic wrap and refrigerate for 12 hours. Remove chicken pieces from pickle brine and pat dry with paper towels.

Set out a large sheet pan. Combine flour, salt, and pepper in a 9 x 13-inch baking pan or other large, shallow pan. Pour buttermilk into another large, shallow pan. Dredge each piece of chicken in seasoned flour, then in buttermilk, and again into the seasoned flour. Set dredged chicken onto the sheet pan as you go. (This can be done up to 2 hours before frying. Refrigerate until ready to fry; bring to room temperature before continuing.)

Preheat oven to 170°F. Line a baking sheet with a paper bag or paper towels and set aside. Pour oil to a depth of 1 inch into a 12-inch (or larger) heavy, straight-sided frying pan and set over medium-high heat. (Beth notes: "I love my big, deep cast iron pans—but my mother always fried her chicken in a 9 x 13-inch electric skillet, and it always turned out great!") When the oil reaches 325°F, start adding the chicken pieces skin side down, 4 pieces at a time (or more if you're using a very large pan, but don't overcrowd the pan).

Fry the chicken for 5 minutes, then take a peek at skin side to check for color and adjust the heat so the chicken is gently browning but not burning. When chicken is golden brown, turn and fry the other side until golden brown. Continue frying and occasionally turning the pieces for a total of 20–30 minutes, or until internal temperature reaches 165°F. Transfer cooked chicken pieces to a clean paper-bag- or paper-towel-lined baking sheet to drain. Place fried pieces in oven while you finish frying the remaining chicken.

In a small bowl, combine pickles with fresh dill. Spoon on top of chicken pieces and serve.

Zen Box Izakaya

602 S. Washington Avenue
Minneapolis, MN 55415
(612) 332-3936
zenboxizakaya.com
General Manager/Co-Owner: Lina Goh
Executive Chef/Co-Owner: John Ng

Like most small children, my son and stepdaughter were big pot-sticker fans. They devoured them whenever we ate at an Asian restaurant, and I marveled at how they could so thoroughly enjoy what were mostly pretty awful dumplings. Every time they asked for them, my then-husband would wince and say that if only they could try the glorious pot stickers he had started grabbing for lunch, from a new spot called Zen Box in the skyway of downtown Minneapolis, they would stop ordering the awful ones. We finally coordinated a giant take-out order of Zen Box for the kids one night, and they were blown away by the tender wrappers, perfectly seasoned filling, and crispy-not-greasy bottoms. That night, a couple of young pot-sticker snobs—and Zen Box fans—were born.

Husband-and-wife team John Ng and Lina Goh took their loyal lunchtime following and their passion for "beyond sushi" Japanese food and launched Zen Box Izakaya near the Guthrie Theater in 2011. While the original Zen Box specialized in bento box lunches, perfect for lunchtime crowds on the go-go-go, the new spot gave Ng and Goh the opportunity to introduce the Twin Cities to the informal, sit-down-and-relax concept of *izakaya*, or Japanese pub culture. An izakaya is a place to drink—sometimes a lot—but to eat a lot, too, lingering over both drinks and food, enjoying a night bawdily laughing with friends. Dishes range from small or large plates of fried, crispy snacks to silky tofus to dumplings and noodles, all engineered to be utterly addictive alongside sake and beer . . . think bar food with Japanese finesse.

Not content to just open an ambitious new restaurant, the couple hosted a giant ramen block party in 2013, followed by a dream trip, eating their way through Japan, sharing the deliciousness—and their contagious enthusiasm for all things food—on social media as they darted from one spot to the next. Ng has been channeling the inspiration gleaned from the visiting ramen block-party chefs as well as the epic trip into a knockout series of ramen specials. Says Ng, "The ability to play and explore with so many ingredients and cooking techniques, through traveling and eating throughout Japan, has been the best part of what we do!" Given there is no better refuge from a brutal

Minnesota winter than the glorious comfort of a fragrant bowl of ramen, there are many happy recipients of their inspiration. Many of Ng's specials have sold out in short order as hungry, freezing Minneapolitans crowd into Zen Box to drink beer and sake, slurp noodles, chat with Ng and Goh, and do their best to survive until spring. *Kampai!*

SHIO RAMEN WITH CHICKEN CHASHU & TEMPURA FOIE GRAS

(MAKES 1 BOWL OF RAMEN)

1 chicken thigh, skinned and boned, skin reserved

Sea salt and freshly ground black pepper

Pinch of shichimi togarashi (optional)

1 teaspoon plus 2 cups vegetable oil for high-heat frying (safflower, peanut, or canola), divided

2 tablespoons chopped garlic

4 square inches kombu kelp

2 cups water, plus more for cooking noodles

⅓ pound cleaned fresh mussels

3 ounces katsuo bushi (bonito flakes)

1¼ cups chicken broth

5 ounces foie gras, sliced into ½-inch-thick slices

1 cup tempura flour

1 cup ice water

1 serving fresh ramen noodles (such as Sun Brand, available locally at United Noodles)

2 ounces mizuna greens (or watercress or arugula leaves)

1 scallion, julienned

To make the chicken chashu: Lightly season chicken thigh with salt, black pepper, and shichimi togarashi. Roll chicken into a cylinder shape and tie with butcher twine.

Fill a large saucepan three-quarters full of salted water. Heat water over medium heat to a simmer. Add chicken to water and turn heat to low, maintaining barely breaking bubbles. Slow-poach chicken thigh for approximately 40 minutes, or until internal temperature reaches 165°F. Transfer thigh to a bowl of ice water and let cool for 10 minutes. Remove from water and set aside.

To make the aroma oil: Add 1 teaspoon vegetable oil to an 8-inch skillet. Set over low heat and, when oil is hot, add chicken skin and garlic and fry until chicken skin is brown and crispy, stirring occasionally, 7–8 minutes. Strain oil into a small bowl and set aside. Discard (or eat!) the chicken skin.

To make the broth: Wipe both sides of kombu kelp with a clean damp cloth. Add 2 cups water to a large saucepan and set over medium-high heat. Add kombu to the pan, bring water to a boil, turn heat to low, and simmer kombu for 15 minutes. Skim foam from surface as kombu simmers. Using tongs, remove kombu from water and discard, leaving water in pan.

Turn heat to high and bring kombu water to a boil. Add mussels to kombu water and boil for 2 minutes, pull pan from heat, add katsuo bushi (bonito flakes) to the pan, cover, and let sit for 15 minutes. Strain broth into a medium saucepan; discard mussels and bonito. Add chicken broth to the mussel broth and set over lowest heat so broth is simmering hot when ready to assemble the ramen.

To make the foie gras tempura: Add oil to a large, deep saucepan and set over medium-high heat.

While oil heats, season foie gras with salt and pepper. In a medium bowl, combine tempura flour and ice water.

When oil reaches 340°F, dip foie gras slices, one at a time, in tempura batter and fry in oil until crispy and golden on both sides, about 4 minutes per side. Remove foie gras from oil and transfer to a paper-towel-lined plate.

To prepare the noodles and serve: Cook noodles per instructions on ramen package (instructions vary by brand).

While water heats and noodles cook, prepare the bowl for serving: Into a large, deep soup bowl, add 1 teaspoon sea salt and a drizzle of the aroma oil. Pour hot chicken/mussel broth into the bowl and stir. When noodles are done, drain and add to the bowl. Top with sliced chicken chashu and tempura foie gras. Garnish with mizuna and scallion. Devour!

Index

About the Author/Photographer

Stephanie A. Meyer is a Minneapolis-based food writer, photographer, cooking instructor, and recipe developer. She writes a popular food blog, *Fresh Tart*, and is a columnist and blogger for *Minnesota Monthly* magazine and *Mother Earth Living*. Meyer's recipes and photographs have appeared in numerous magazines, cookbooks, and websites, including *Food & Wine, Cambria Style*, and *Edible Twin Cities*. She is the founder and organizer of Fortify: A Food Community, a group of Minnesota food writers and industry professionals who host educational events and raise money for local charities.

Meyer is a self-taught food photographer, inspired to share the simplicity and healthfulness of home cooking. Her approachable, flavorful recipes and beautiful, simple photography get people into their kitchens and cooking from scratch. A whole, fresh food advocate, Meyer's next project will focus on grain-free cooking.